1821: WHALE-SHIP 'ESSEX'

OWEN CHASE

Edited with
an introduction by
Jacqueline Tobin

www.hugejam.com

First published 1821 by W B Gilley

This edition © Huge Jam Publishing 2016
All rights reserved.

ISBN: 978-1-911249-00-9

"This manuscript will doubtless afford you the greatest pleasure; but to me, who know him and hear it from his own lips – with what interest and sympathy shall I read it in some future day! Even now, as I commence my task ... I see his thin hand raised in animation, while the lineaments of his face are irradiated by the soul within. Strange and harrowing must be his story, frightful the storm which embraced the gallant vessel on its course and wrecked it – thus!"

Mary Shelley, 'Frankenstein', Letter 4

CONTENTS

Editor's introduction	i
Author's introduction	iii
Part 1	1
Part 2	7
Part 3	19
Appendices	73

EDITOR'S INTRODUCTION, 2016

> No wonder Ocean was still mysterious, when such red hearts beat in it! No wonder man, with his tragedy, was a pale and sickly thing in comparison!
> *D H Lawrence 'The Flying Fish'*

Two accounts have predominantly served as sources not just for Philbrick's 'In The Heart of The Sea' but also for Melville's 'Moby Dick', and for other less famous narratives. This book is one of those sources. Melville was handed a copy of it by Owen Chase's son when they were both young whalers. The other, by Thomas Nickerson who was a cabin boy on the *Essex*, was not published until 1984.

Many express a preference for Nickerson's more dynamic writing style. I am among those readers who find more terror in Chase's stark realism. Events that are recounted in the diary you are about to read need nothing more than the honest and vivid description Chase supplies. His directness is either chilling or moving depending upon the events that befall the crew on various days. Devoid of melodrama and sentimentality the story reads all the more powerfully.

Not that his writing is without elegance and poetry. From incidental descriptions such as the rain being 'preceded by sharp flashes of lightning, that appeared to wrap our little barge in flames', to his conveyance of intense emotion, to the Gothic horror that develops as the ordeal continues, Chase controls his words as masterfully as he controls his impulse to despair. His description of the attack is breathtaking.

I suggest that in part his talent stems from his very intelligent self-awareness, even self-consciousness, and his desire to do what is right. This lends to the writing a 'meta-narrative', an expanded perspective. In places it might even be said to foreshadow modern ideas of the 'self' in literature: there's even a bit of Carraway in it. His relief at having survived is contained somewhat by this self-consciousness: 'the ragged remnants of clothes stuck about our sun-burnt bodies, must have produced an appearance to him affecting and revolting'; and his angst did not leave him: 'It has appeared to me often since to have been, in the abstract, an extreme weakness and folly, on our parts, to have looked upon our shattered and sunken vessel with such an excessive fondness and regret …'

It is due to the genuine horror of the events Chase and the crew experienced that even though this narrative is filled with examples of courage, discipline and occasionally optimism, what one takes from it and cannot shake off is the Gothic element. Covering with sheets the bodies of those who had willed themselves to die or succumbed to madness, descriptions of the men's cadaverous appearance, and the strips of human flesh waving in the air (even cannibalism is dignified by powerful description: 'Humanity must shudder at the dreadful recital. I have no language to paint the anguish of our souls in this dreadful dilemma.') are frighteningly vivid. I have chosen to include extracts from Shelley's 'Frankenstein' and Coleridge's 'Rime of The Ancient Mariner', texts with which Chase might have been familiar, in an appendix.

Aged 23 at the time, Chase lived until he was 71. Although he went on to captain several ships, he stopped work in his forties due to ill-health brought on by his *Essex* experience. I ought here to note that Herman Melville believed that Chase's story was ghost-written for him, based on his narration from nine scraps of paper upon which he had kept notes. The story was not widely read and not reprinted.

A further note on the text: this edition differs from others in that Chase's writing has been formatted into paragraphs. Paragraphs do not feature in the original and for many this has detracted from the pleasure of reading. Words have not been altered. It is the complete and unabridged text.

Jac Tobin, January 2nd 2016

CHASE'S INTRODUCTION, 1821

To the reader

I am aware that the public mind has been already nearly sated with the private stories of individuals, many of whom had few, if any, claims to public attention, and the injuries which have resulted from the promulgation of fictitious histories, and in many instances, of journals entirely fabricated for the purpose, has had the effect to lessen the public interest in works of this description, and very much to undervalue the general cause of truth. It is, however, not the less important and necessary, that narratives should continue to be furnished that have their foundation in fact, and the subject of which embraces new and interesting matter in any department of the arts or sciences.

When the motive is worthy, the subject and style interesting, affording instruction, exciting a proper sympathy, and withal disclosing new and astonishing traits of human character – this kind of information becomes of great value to the philanthropist and philosopher, and is fully deserving of attention from every description of readers.

On the subject of the facts contained in this little volume, they are neither so extravagant, as to require the exercise of any great credulity to believe, nor, I trust, so unimportant or uninteresting, as to forbid an attentive perusal. It was my misfortune to be a considerable, if not a principal, sufferer, in the dreadful catastrophe that befell us; and in it, I not only lost all the little I had ventured, but my situation and the prospects of bettering it, that at one time seemed to smile upon me, were all in one short moment destroyed with it. The hope of obtaining something of remuneration, by giving a short history of my sufferings to the world, must therefore constitute my claim to public attention.

PART ONE

The town of Nantucket, in the State of Massachusetts, contains about eight thousand inhabitants; nearly a third part of the population are quakers, and they are, taken together, a very industrious and enterprising people. On this island are owned about one hundred vessels, of all descriptions, engaged in the whale trade, giving constant employment and support to upwards of sixteen hundred hardy seaman, a class of people proverbial for their intrepidity. This fishery is not carried on to any extent from any other part of the United States, except from the town of New Bedford, directly opposite to Nantucket, where are owned probably twenty sail.

A voyage generally lasts about two years and a half, and with an entire uncertainty of success. Sometimes they are repaid with speedy voyages and profitable cargoes, and at others they drag out a listless and disheartening cruise, without scarcely making the expenses of an outfit. The business is considered a very hazardous one, arising from unavoidable accidents, in carrying on an exterminating warfare against those great leviathans of the deep; and indeed a Nantucket man is on all occasions fully sensible of the honour and merit of his profession; no doubt because he knows that his laurels, like the soldier's, are plucked from the brink of danger. Numerous anecdotes are related of the whalemen of Nantucket; and stories of hair-breadth 'scapes, and sudden and wonderful preservation, are handed down amongst them, with the fidelity, and no doubt many of them with the characteristic fictions of the ancient legendary tales.

A spirit of adventure amongst the sons of other relatives of these immediately concerned in it, takes possession of their minds at an early age; captivated with the tough stories of the elder seamen, and seduced, as well as the natural desire of seeing foreign countries, as by the hopes of gain, they launch forth six or eight thousand miles from home, into years of their lives in scenes of constant peril, labour, and watchfulness.

The profession is one of great ambition, and full of honourable excitement: a tame man is never known amongst them; and the coward is marked with that peculiar aversion, that distinguishes our public naval service. There are perhaps no people of superior corporeal powers; and it has been truly said of them, that they possess a natural aptitude, which seems rather the lineal spirit of their fathers, than the effects of any experience.

The town itself, during the war, was (naturally to have been expected) on the decline; but with the return of peace it took a fresh start, and a spirit for carrying on the fishery received a renewed and very considerable excitement. Large capitals are now embarked; and some of the finest ships that our country can boast of are employed in it. The increased demand, within a few years past, from the spermaceti manufactories, has induced companies and individuals in different parts of the Union to become engaged in the business; and if the future consumption of the manufactured article bear any proportion to that of the few past years, this species of commerce will bid fair to become the most profitable and extensive that our country possesses.

From the accounts of those who were in the early stages of the fishery concerned it, it would appear, that the whales have been driven, like the beasts of the forest, before the march of civilization, into remote and more unfrequented seas, until now, they are followed by the enterprise and perseverance of our seamen, even to the distant coasts of Japan.

The ship Essex, commanded by captain George Pollard, junior, was fitted out at Nantucket, and sailed on the 12th day of August, 1819, for the Pacific Ocean, on a whaling voyage. Of this ship I was first mate. She had lately undergone a thorough repair in her upper works, and was at that time, in all respects, a sound, substantial vessel: she had a crew of twenty-one men, and was victualled and provided for two years and a half.

We left the coast of America with a fine breeze, and steered for the Western Islands. On the second day out, while sailing moderately on our course in the Gulf Stream, a sudden squall of wind struck the ship from the SW, and knocked her completely on her beam-ends, stove one of our boats, entirely destroyed two others, and threw down the cambouse. We distinctly saw the approach of this gust, but miscalculated altogether as to the strength and violence of it. It struck the ship about three points off the weather quarter, at the moment that the man at the helm was in the act of putting her away to run before it. In an instant she was knocked down with her yards in the water; and before hardly a moment of time was allowed for reflection, she gradually came to the wind, and righted.

The squall was accompanied with vivid flashes of lighting, and heavy and repeated claps of thunder. The whole ship's crew were, for a short time, throws into the utmost consternation and confusion; but fortunately the violence of the squall was all contained in the first gust of the wind, and it soon gradually abated, and became fine weather again.

We repaired our damage with little difficulty, and continued on our course, with the loss of the two boats. On the 30th of August we made the island of Floros, one of the western group called the Azores. We lay off and on the island for two days, during which time our boats landed and obtained a supply of vegetables and a few hogs: from this place we took the NE trade-wind, and in sixteen days made the Isle of May, one of the Cape de Verdes.

As we were sailing along the shore of this island, we discovered a ship stranded on the beach, and from her appearance took her to be a whaler, Having lost two of our boats, and presuming that this vessel had probably some belonging to her that might have been saved, we determined to ascertain the name of the ship, and endeavor to supply if possible the loss of our boats from her. We accordingly stood in towards the port, or landing place.

After a short time three men were discovered coming out to us in a whale boat. In a few moments they were alongside, and informed us that the wreck was the Archimedes of New York, captain George B. Coffin, which vessel had struck on a rock near the island about a fortnight previously; that all hands were saved by running the ship on shore, and that the captain and crew had gone home. We purchased the whale boat of these people, obtained some few more pigs, and again set sail.

Our passage thence to Cape Horn was not distinguished for any incident worthy of note. We made the longitude of the Cape about the 18th of December, having experienced head winds for nearly the whole distance. We anticipated a moderate time in passing this noted land, from the season of the year at which we were there, being considered the most favourable; but instead of this, we experienced heavy westerly gales, and a most tremendous sea, that detained us off the Cape five weeks, before we had got sufficiently to the westward to enable us to put away. Of the passage of this famous Cape it may be observed, that strong westerly gales and a heavy sea are its almost universal attendants: the prevalence and constancy of this wind and sea necessarily produce a rapid current, by which vessels are set to leeward; and it is not without some favourable slant of wind that they can in many cases get round at all. The difficulties and dangers of the passage are proverbial; but as far as my own observation extends (and which the numerous reports of the whalemen corroborate), you can always rely upon a long and regular sea; and although the gales may be very strong and stubborn, as they undoubtedly are, they are not known to blow with the destructive violence that characterizes some of the tornadoes of the western Atlantic Ocean.

On the 17th of January, 1820, we arrived at the island of St. Mary's lying on the coast of Chile, in latitude 36°59' S. longitude 73°41' W. 8. This island is a sort of rendezvous for whalers, from which they obtain their wood and water, and between which and the main land (a distance of about ten miles) they frequently cruise for a species of whale called the right whale. Our object in going in there was merely to get the news. We sailed thence to the island of Massafuera, where we got some wood and fish, and thence for the cruising ground along the coast of Chile, in search of the spermaceti whale. We took there eight, which yielded us two hundred and fifty barrels of oil; and the season having by this time expired, we changed our cruising ground to the coast of Peru. We obtained there five hundred and fifty barrels. After going into the small port of Decamas, and replenishing our wood and water, on the 2nd of October we set sail for the Galapagos Islands.

We came to anchor, and laid seven days off Hood's Island, one of the group; during which time we stopped a leak which we had discovered, and obtained three hundred turtle. We then visited Charles Island, where we procured sixty more. These turtle are a most delicious food, and average in weight generally about one hundred pounds, but many of them weigh upwards of eight hundred. With these, ships usually supply themselves for a great length of time and make a great saving of other provisions. They neither eat nor drink, nor is the least pains taken with them; they are strewed over the deck, thrown underfoot, or packed away in the hold, as it suits convenience. They will live upwards of a year without food or water, but soon die in a cold climate.

We left Charles Island on the 23rd of October, and steered off to the westward, in search of whales. In latitude 1°0' S. longitude 118° W. on the 16th of November, in the afternoon, we lost a boat during our work in a shoal of whales. I was in the boat myself, with five others, and was standing in the fore part, with the harpoon in my hand, well braced, expecting every instant to catch sight of one of the shoal which we were in, that I might strike; but judge of my astonishment and dismay, at finding myself suddenly thrown up in the air, my companions scattered about me, and the boat fast filling with water.

A whale had come up directly under her, and with one dash of his tail, had stove her bottom in, and strewed us in every direction around her. We, however, with little difficulty, got safely on the wreck, and clung there until one of the other boats which had been engaged in the shoal, came to our assistance, and took us off.

Strange to tell, not a man was injured by this accident. Thus it happens very frequently in the whaling business, that boats are stove; oars, harpoons, and lines broken; ankles and wrists sprained; boats upset, and whole crews left for hours in the water, without any of these accidents extending to the loss of life.

We are so much accustomed to the continual recurrence of such scenes as these, that we become familiarized to them, and consequently always feel that confidence and self-possession, which teaches us every expedient in danger, and inures the body, as well as the mind, to fatigue, privation, and peril, in frequent cases exceeding belief.

It is this danger and hardship that makes the sailor; indeed it is the distinguishing qualification amongst us; and it is a common boast of the whaleman, that he has escaped from sudden and apparently inevitable destruction oftener than his fellow. He is accordingly valued on this account, without much reference to other qualities.

PART TWO

I have not been able to recur to the scenes which are now to become the subject of description, although a considerable time has elapsed without feeling a mingled emotion of horror and astonishment at the almost incredible destiny that has preserved me and my surviving companions from a terrible death.

Frequently, in my reflections on the subject, even after this lapse of time, I find myself shedding tears of gratitude for our deliverance, and blessing God, by whose divine aid and protection we were conducted through a series of unparalleled suffering and distress, and restored to the bosoms of our families and friends.

There is no knowing what a stretch of pain and misery the human mind is capable of contemplating, when it is wrought upon by the anxieties of preservation; nor what pangs and weaknesses the body is able to endure, until they are visited upon it; and when at last deliverance comes, when the dream of hope is realized, unspeakable gratitude takes possession of the soul, and tears of joy choke the utterance. We require to be taught in the school of some signal suffering, privation, and despair, the great lessons of constant dependence upon an almighty forbearance and mercy.

In the midst of the wide ocean, at night, when the sight of the heavens was shut out, and the dark tempest came upon us; then it was, that we felt ourselves ready to exclaim, "Heaven have mercy upon us, for nought but that can save us now." But I proceed to the recital.

– On the 20th of November (cruising in latitude 0°40' S. longitude 71.19°0' W.), a shoal of whales was discovered off the leebow. The weather at this time was extremely fine and clear, and it was about 8 o'clock in the morning, that the man at the mast-head gave the usual cry of, "There she blows." The ship was immediately put away, and we ran down in the direction for them.

When we had got within half a mile of the place where they were observed, all our boats were lowered down, manned, and we started in pursuit of them. The ship, in the meantime, was brought to the wind, and the main-top-sail hove aback, to wait for us. I had the harpoon in the second boat; the captain preceded me in the first.

When I arrived at the spot where we calculated they were, nothing was at first to be seen. We lay on our oars in anxious expectation of discovering them come up somewhere near us. Presently one rose, and spouted a short distance ahead of my boat; I made all speed towards it, came up with, and struck it; feeling the harpoon in him, he threw himself, in an agony, over towards the boat (which at that time was up alongside of him), and giving a severe blow with his tail, struck the boat near the edge of the water, amidships, and stove a hole in her.

I immediately took up the boat hatchet, and cut the line, to disengage the boat from the whale, which by this time was running off with great velocity. I succeeded in getting clear of him, with the loss of the harpoon and line; and finding the water to pour fast in the boat. I hastily stuffed three or four of our jackets in the hole, ordered one man to keep constantly bailing, and the rest to pull immediately for the ship; we succeeded in keeping the boat free, and shortly gained the ship. The captain and the second mate, in the other two boats, kept up the pursuit, and soon struck another whale. They being at this time a considerable distance to leeward, I went forward, braced around the mainyard, and put the ship off in a direction for them; the boat which had been stove was immediately hoisted in, and after examining the hole, I found that I could, by nailing a piece of canvass over it, get her ready to join in a fresh pursuit, sooner than by lowering down the other remaining boat which belonged to the ship.

I accordingly turned her over upon the quarter, and was in the act of nailing on the canvass, when I observed a very large spermaceti whale, as well as I could judge, about eighty-five feet in length; he broke water about twenty rods off our weather-bow, and was lying quietly, with his head in a direction for the ship. He spouted two or three times, and then disappeared.

In less than two or three seconds he came up again, about the length of the ship off, and made directly for us, at the rate of about three knots. The ship was then going with about the same velocity. His appearance and attitude gave us at first no alarm; but while I stood watching his movements, and observing him but a ship's length off, coming down for us with great celerity, I involuntarily ordered the boy at the helm to put it hard up; intending to sheer off and avoid him.

The words were scarcely out of my mouth, before he came down upon us with full speed, and struck the ship with his head, just forward of the fore-chains; he gave us such an appalling and tremendous jar, as nearly threw us all on our faces.

The ship brought up as suddenly and violently as if she had struck a rock and trembled for a few seconds like a leaf. We looked at each other with perfect amazement, deprived almost of the power of speech.

Many minutes elapsed before we were able to realize the dreadful accident; during which time he passed under the ship, grazing her keel as he went along, came up underside of her to leeward, and lay on the top of the water (apparently stunned with the violence of the blow), for the space of a minute; he then suddenly started off, in a direction to leeward.

After a few moments' reflection, and recovering, in some measure, from the sudden consternation that had seized us, I of course concluded that he had stove a hole in the ship, and that it would be necessary to set the pumps going. Accordingly they were rigged, but had not been in operation more than one minute, before I perceived the head of the ship to be gradually settling down in the water; I then ordered the signal to be set for the other boats, which scarcely had I dispatched, before I again discovered the whale, apparently in convulsions, on the top of the water, about one hundred rods to leeward. He was enveloped in the foam of the sea, that his continual and violent thrashing about in the water had created around him, and I could distinctly see him smite his jaws together, as if distracted with rage and fury. He remained a short time in this situation, and then started off with great velocity, across the bows of the ship, to windward.

By this time the ship had settled down a considerable distance in the water, and I gave her up as lost. I however, ordered the pumps to be kept constantly going, and endeavoured to collect my thoughts for the occasion. I turned to the boats, two of which we then had with the ship, with an intention of clearing them away, and getting all things ready to embark in them, if there should be no other resource left; and while my attention was thus engaged for a moment, I was aroused with the cry of a man at the hatchway, "Here he is – he is making for us again."

I turned around, and saw him about one hundred rods directly ahead of us, coming down apparently with twice his ordinary speed, and to me at that moment, it appeared with tenfold fury and vengeance in his aspect. The surf flew in all directions about him, and his course towards us was marked by a white foam of a rod in width, which he made with the continual violent thrashing of his tail; his head was about half out of water, and in that way he came upon, and again struck the ship.

I was in hopes when I descried him making for us, that by a dexterous movement of putting the ship away immediately, I should be able to cross the line of his approach, before he could get up to us, and thus avoid, what I knew, if he should strike us again, would prove our inevitable destruction.

I bawled out to the helmsman, "hard up!" but she had not fallen off more than a point, before we took the second shock.

I should judge the speed of the ship to have been at this time about three knots, and that of the whale about six. He struck her to windward, directly under the cathead, and completely stove in her bows. He passed under the ship again, went off to leeward, and we saw no more of him.

Our situation at this juncture can be more readily imagined than described. The shock to our feelings was such, as I am sure none can have an adequate conception of, that were not there: the misfortune befell us at a moment when we least dreamt of any accident; and from the pleasing anticipations we had formed, of realizing the certain profits of our labour, we were dejected by a sudden, most mysterious, and overwhelming calamity.

Not a moment, however, was to be lost in endeavouring to provide for the extremity to which it was now certain we were reduced. We were more than a thousand miles from the nearest land, and with nothing but a light open boat, as the resource of safety for myself and companions. I ordered the men to cease pumping, and every one to provide for himself, seizing a hatchet at the same time, I cut away the lashings of the spare boat, which lay bottom up, across two spars directly over the quarter deck, and cried out to those near me, to take her as she came down. They did so accordingly, and bore her on their shoulders as far as the waist of the ship.

The steward had in the meantime gone down into the cabin twice, and saved two quadrants, two practical navigators, and the captain's trunk and mine; all which were hastily thrown into the boat, as she lay on the deck, with the two compasses which I snatched from the binnacle. He attempted to descend again; but the water by this time had rushed in, and he returned without being able to effect his purpose.

By the time we had got the boat to the waist, the ship had filled with water, and was going down on her beam-ends: we shoved our boat as quickly as possible from the plant-shear into the water, all hands jumping in her at the same time, and launched off clear of the ship. We were scarcely two boats' lengths distant from her, when she fell over to windward, and settled down in the water.

Amazement and despair now wholly took possession of us. We contemplated the frightful situation the ship lay in, and thought with horror upon the sudden and dreadful calamity that had overtaken us. We looked upon each other, as if to gather some consolatory sensation from an interchange of sentiments, but every countenance was marked with the paleness of despair. Not a word was spoken for several minutes by any of us; all appeared to be bound in a spell of stupid consternation; and from the time we were first attacked by the whale, to the period of the fall of the ship, and of our leaving her in the boat, more than ten minutes could not certainly have elapsed! God only knows in what way, or by what means, we were enabled to accomplish in that short time what we did, the cutting away and transporting the boat from where she was deposited would of itself, in ordinary circumstances, have consumed as much time as that if the whole ship's crew had been employed in it.

My companions had not saved a single article but what they had on their backs; but to me it was a source of infinite satisfaction, if any such could be gathered from the horrors of our gloomy situation, that we had been fortunate enough to have preserved our compasses, navigators, and quadrants.

After the first shock of my feelings was over, I enthusiastically contemplated them as the probable instruments of our salvation; without them all would have been dark and hopeless.

Gracious God! What a picture of distress and suffering now presented itself to my imagination. The crew of the ship were saved, consisting of twenty human souls. All that remained to conduct these twenty beings through the stormy terrors of the ocean, perhaps many thousand miles, were three open light boats.

The prospect of obtaining any provisions or water from the ship, to subsist upon during the time, was at least now doubtful. How many long and watchful nights, thought I, are to be passed? How many tedious days of partial starvation are to be endured, before the least relief of mitigation of our sufferings can be reasonably anticipated? We lay at this time in our boat, about two ship's lengths off from the wreck, in perfect silence, calmly contemplating her situation, and absorbed in our own melancholy reflections, when the other boats were discovered rowing up to us. They had but shortly before discovered that some accident had befallen us, but of the nature of which they were entirely ignorant. The sudden and mysterious disappearance of the ship was first discovered by the boat-steerer in the captain's boat, and with a horror-struck countenance and voice, he suddenly exclaimed, "Oh, my God! Where is the Ship?"

Their operations upon this were instantly suspended, and a general cry of horror and despair burst from the lips of every man, as their looks were directed for her, in vain, over every part of the ocean. They immediately made all haste towards us.

The captain's boat was the first that reached us. He stopped about a boat's length off, but had no power to utter a single syllable: he was so completely overpowered with the spectacle before him, that he sat down in his boat, pale and speechless. I could scarely recognize his countenance, he appeared to be so much altered, awed, and overcome, with the oppression of his feelings, and the dreadful reality that lay before him.

He was in a short time however enabled to address the inquiry to me, "My God, Mr. Chase, what is the matter?" I answered, "We have been stove by a whale." I then briefly told him the story. After a few moment's reflection he observed, that we must cut away her masts, and endeavour to get something out of her to eat.

Our thoughts were now all accordingly bent on endeavours to save from the wreck whatever we might possibly want, and for this purpose we rowed up and got on to her. Search was made for every means of gaining access to her hold; and for this purpose the lanyards were cut loose, and with our hatchets we commenced to cut away the masts, that she might right up again, and enable us to scuttle her decks. In doing which we were occupied about three quarters of an hour owing to our having no axes, nor indeed any other instructions, but the small hatchets belonging to the boats.

After her masts were gone she came up about two-thirds of the way upon an even keel. While we were employed about the masts the captain took his quadrant, shoved off the ship, and got an observation. We found ourselves in latitude 0°40' S. longitude 119° W.

We now commenced to cut a hole through the planks, directly above two large casks of bread, which most fortunately were between decks, in the waist of the ship, and which being in the upper side, when she upset, we had strong hopes was not wet. It turned out according to our wishes, and from these casks we obtained six hundred pounds of hard bread. Other parts of the deck were then scuttled, and we got without difficulty as much fresh water as we dared to take in the boats, so that each was supplied with about sixty-five gallons; we got also from one of the lockers a musket, a small canister of powder, a couple of files, two rasps, about two pounds of boat nails, and a few turtle.

In the afternoon the wind came on to blow a strong breeze; and having obtained everything that occurred to us could then be got out, we began to make arrangements for our safety during the night. A boat's line was made fast to the ship, and to the other end of it one of the boats was moored; at about fifty fathoms to leeward; another boat was then attached to the first one, about eight fathoms astern; and the third boat, the like distance astern of her.

Night came on just as we had finished our operations; and such a night as it was to us! So full of feverish and distracting inquietude, that we were deprived entirely of rest. The wreck was constantly before my eyes. I could not, by any effort, chase away the horrors of the preceding day from my mind: they haunted me the live-long night. My companions – some of them were like sick women; they had no idea of the extent of their deplorable situation. One or two slept unconcernedly, while others wasted the night in unavailing murmurs.

I now had full leisure to examine, with some degree of coolness, the dreadful circumstances of our disaster. The scenes of yesterday passed in such quick succession in my mind that it was not until after many hours of severe reflection that I was able to discard the idea of the catastrophe as a dream.

Alas! It was one from which there was no awaking; it was too certainly true, that but yesterday we had existed as it were, and in one short moment had been cut off from the hopes and prospects of the living! I have no language to paint out the horrors of our situation. To shed tears was indeed altogether unavailing, and withal unmanly; yet I was not able to deny myself the relief they served to afford me.

After several hours of idle sorrow and repining I began to reflect upon the accident, and endeavoured to realize by what unaccountable destiny or design (which I could not at first determine), this sudden and most deadly attack had been made upon us: by an animal, too, never before suspected of premeditated violence, and proverbial for its insensibility and inoffensiveness.

Every fact seemed to warrant me in concluding that it was anything but chance which directed his operations; he made two several attacks upon the ship, at a short interval between them, both of which, according to their direction, were calculated to do us the most injury, by being made ahead, and thereby combining the speed of the two objects for the shock; to effect which, the exact manoeuvres which he made were necessary.

His aspect was most horrible, and such as indicated resentment and fury. He came directly from the shoal which we had just before entered, and in which we had struck three of his companions, as if fired with revenge for their sufferings.

But to this it may be observed, that the mode of fighting which they always adopt is either with repeated strokes of their tails, or snapping of their jaws together; and that a case, precisely similar to this one, has never been heard of amongst the oldest and most experienced whalers.

To this I would answer, that the structure and strength of the whale's head is admirably designed for this mode of attack; the most prominent part of which is almost as hard and as tough as iron; indeed, I can compare it to nothing else but the inside of a horse's hoof, upon which a lance or harpoon would not make the slightest impression. The eyes and ears are removed nearly one-third the length of the whole fish, from the front part of the head, and are not in the least degree endangered in this mode of attack.

Nickerson's sketch from the day of the attack, courtesy of the Nantucket Historical Association

At all events, the whole circumstances taken together, all happening before my own eyes, and producing, at the time, impressions in my mind of decided, calculated mischief, on the part of the whale (many of which impressions I cannot now recall), induce me to be satisfied that I am correct in my opinion.

It is certainly, in all its bearings, a hitherto unheard of circumstance, and constitutes, perhaps, the most extraordinary one in the annals of the fishery.

PART THREE

November 21st

The morning dawned upon our wretched company. The weather was fine, but the wind blew a strong breeze from the SE, and the sea was very rugged. Watches had been kept up during the night, in our respective boats, to see that none of the spars or other articles (which continued to float out of the wreck) should be thrown by the surf against, and injure the boats.

At sunrise, we began to think of doing something; what, we did not know; we cast loose our boats, and visited the wreck, to see if anything more of consequence could be preserved, but everything looked cheerless and desolate, and we made a long and vain search for any useful article; nothing could be found but a few turtle; of these we had enough already; or at least, as many as could be safely stowed in the boats, and we wandered around in every part of the ship in a sort of vacant idleness for the greater part of the morning.

We were presently aroused to a perfect sense of our destitute and forlorn condition, by thoughts of the means which we had for our subsistence, the necessity of not wasting our time, and of endeavouring to seek some relief wherever God might direct us. Our thoughts, indeed, hung about the ship, wrecked and sunken as she was, and we could scarcely discard from our minds the idea of her continuing protection. Some great efforts in our situation were necessary, and a great deal of calculation important, as it concerned by the means by which our existence was to be supported during, perhaps, a very long period, and a provision for our eventual deliverance. Accordingly, by agreement, all set to work in stripping off the light sails of the ship, for sails to our boats; and the day was consumed in making them up and fitting them. We furnished ourselves with masts and other light spars that were necessary, from the wreck. Each boat was rigged with two masts, to carry a flying-jib and two spirit-sails; the spirit-sails were made so that two reefs could be taken in them, in case of heavy blows. We continued to watch the wreck for any serviceable articles that might float from her, and kept one man during the day, on the stump of her foremast, on the look out for vessels.

Our work was very much impeded by the increase of the wind and sea, and the surf breaking almost continually into the boats, gave us many fears that we should not be able to prevent our provisions from getting wet; and above all served to increase the constant apprehensions that we had, of the insufficiency of the boats themselves, during the rough weather that we should necessarily experience. In order to provide as much as possible against this, and withal to strengthen the slight materials of which the boats were constructed, we procured from the wreck some light cedar boards (intended to repair boats in case of accidents), with which we built up additional sides, about six inches above the gunwale; these, we afterwards found, were of infinite service for the purpose for which they were intended; in truth, I am satisfied we could never have been preserved without them; the boats must otherwise have taken in so much water that all the efforts of twenty such weak, starving men as we afterwards came to be, would not have sufficed to keep her free; but what appeared most immediately to concern us, and to command all our anxieties, was the security of our provisions from the salt water. We disposed of them under a covering of wood, that whale-boats have at either end of them, wrapping it up in several thicknesses of canvass.

I got an observation to-day, by which I found we were in latitude 0°6' S. longitude 119°30' W. having been driven by the winds a distance of forty-nine miles the last twenty-four hours; by this it would appear that there must have been a strong current, setting us to the NW during the whole time. We were not able to finish our sails in one day; and many little things preparatory to taking a final leave of the ship were necessary to be attended to, but evening came and put an end to our labours.

We made the same arrangements for mooring the boats in safety, and consigned ourselves to the horrors of another tempestuous night. The wind continued to blow hard, keeping up a heavy sea, and veering around from SE to E, and E.SE. As the gloom of night approached, and obliged us to desist from that employment, which cheated us out of some of the realities of our situation, we all of us again became mute and desponding: a considerable degree of alacrity had been manifested by many the preceding day, as their attention had been wholly engaged in scrutinizing the wreck, and in constructing the sails and spars for the boats; but when they ceased to be occupied, they passed to a sudden fit of melancholy, and the miseries of their situation came upon them with such force, as to produce spells of extreme debility, approaching almost to fainting. Our provisions were scarcely touched – the appetite was entirely gone; but as we had a great abundance of water, we indulged in frequent and copious draughts, which our parched mouths seemed continually to need. None asked for bread.

Our continued state of anxiety during the night, excluded all hopes of sleep; still (although the solemn fact had been before me for nearly two days), my mind manifested the utmost repugnance to be reconciled to it; I laid down in the bottom of the boat, and resigned myself to reflection; my silent prayers were offered up to the God of mercy, for that protection which we stood so much in need of. Sometimes, indeed, a light hope would dawn, but then, to feel such an utter dependence on and consignment to chance alone for aid and rescue, would chase it again from my mind. The wreck – the mysterious and mortal attack of the animal – the sudden prostration and sinking of the vessel – our escape from her, and our then forlorn and almost hapless destiny, all passed in quick and perplexing review in my imagination; wearied with the exertion of the body and mind, I caught, near morning, an hour's respite from my troubles, in sleep.

November 22nd

The wind remained the same, and the weather continued remarkably fine. At sunrise, we again hauled our boats up, and continued our search for articles that might float out. About 7 o'clock, the deck of the wreck began to give way, and every appearance indicated her speedy dissolution; the oil had bilged in the hold, and kept the surface of the sea all around us completely covered with it; the bulk-heads were all washed down, and she worked in every part of her joints and seams, with the violent and continual breaking of the surf over her.

Seeing, at last, that little or nothing further could be done by remaining with the wreck, and as it was all important that while our provisions lasted, we should make the best possible use of time, I rowed up to the captain's boat, and asked him what he intended to do. I informed him that the ship's decks had bursted up, and that in all probability she would soon go to pieces; that no further purpose could be answered, by remaining longer with her, since nothing more could be obtained from her; and that it was my opinion, no time should be lost in making the best of our way towards the nearest land.

The captain observed, that he would go once more to the wreck, and survey her, and after waiting until 12 o'clock for the purpose of getting an observation, would immediately after determine.

In the meantime, before noon all our sails were completed, and the boats otherwise got in readiness for our departure. Our observation now proved us to be in latitude 0°13' N. longitude 120°00' W. as near as we could determine it, having crossed the equator during the night, and drifted nineteen miles. The wind had veered considerably to the eastward, during the last twenty-four hours. Our nautical calculations having been completed, the captain, after visiting the wreck, called a council, consisting of himself and the first and second mates, who all repaired to his boat, to interchange opinions, and devise the best means for our security and preservation.

There were, in all of us, twenty men; six of whom were blacks, and we had three boats. We examined our navigators, to ascertain the nearest land, and found it was the Marquesas Islands. The Society Islands were next; these islands we were entirely ignorant of; if inhabited, we presumed they were by savages, from whom we had as much to fear, as from the elements, or even death itself. We had no charts from which our calculations might be aided, and were consequently obliged to govern ourselves by the navigators alone; it was also the captain's opinion, that this was the season of the hurricanes which prevail in the vicinity of the Sandwich Islands, and that consequently it would be unsafe to steer for them. The issue of our deliberations was, that, taking all things into consideration, it would be most advisable to shape our course by the wind, to the southward, as far as 25° or 26° S. latitude, fall in with the variable winds, and then, endeavour to get eastward to the coast of Chile or Peru.

Accordingly, preparations were made for our immediate departure; the boast which it was my fortune, or rather misfortune to have, was the worst of the three; she was old and patched up, having been stove a number of times, during the cruise. At best, a whale-boat is an extremely frail thing; the most so of any other kind of boat; they are what is called clinker built, and constructed of the lightest materials, for the purpose of being rowed with the greatest possible celerity, according to the necessities of the business for which they are intended. Of all species of vessels, they are the weakest, and most fragile, and possess but one advantage over any other – that of lightness and buoyancy, that enables them to keep above the dash of the sea, with more facility than heavier ones. This qualification is, however, preferable to that of any other, and, situated as we then were, I would not have exchanged her, old and crazy as she was, for even a ship's launch. I am quite confident, that to this quality of our boats we most especially owed our preservation, through the many days and nights of heavy weather, that we afterwards encountered. In consideration of my having the weakest boat; six men were allotted to it; while those of the captain and second mate, took seven each; and at half past 12 we left the wreck, steering our course, with nearly all sail set, S.SE. At four o'clock, in the afternoon we lost sight of her entirely. Many were the lingering and sorrowful looks we cast behind us.

It has appeared to me often since to have been, in the abstract, an extreme weakness and folly, on our parts, to have looked upon our shattered and sunken vessel with such an excessive fondness and regret; but it seemed as if in abandoning her we had parted with all hope, and were bending our course away from her, rather by some dictate of despair. We agreed to keep together, in our boats, as nearly as possible to afford assistance in cases of accident, and to render our reflections less melancholy by each other's presence.

I found it on this occasion true, that misery does indeed love company; unaided, and unencouraged by each other, there were with us many whose weak minds, I am confident, would have sunk under the dismal retrospections of the past catastrophe, and who did not possess either sense or firmness enough to contemplate our approaching destiny, without the cheering of some more determined countenance than their own.

The wind was strong all day; and the sea ran very high, our boat taking in water from her leaks continually, so that we were obliged to keep one man constantly bailing. During the night the weather became extremely rugged, and the sea every now and then broke over us. By agreement, we were divided into two watches; one of which was to be constantly awake, and doing the labours of the boat, such as bailing; setting, taking in, and trimming the sails. We kept our course very well together during this night, and had many opportunities of conversation with the men in the other boats, wherein the means and prospects of our deliverance were variously considered; it appeared from the opinions of all, that we had most to hope for in the meeting with some vessel, and most probably some whale ship, the great majority of whom, in those seas, we imagined were cruising about the latitude we were then steering for; but this was only a hope, the realization of which did not in any degree depend on our own exertions, but on chance alone.

It was not, therefore, considered prudent, by going out of our course, with the prospect of meeting them, to lose sight, for one moment, of the strong probabilities which, under Divine providence, there were of our reaching land by the route we had prescribed to ourselves; as that depended, most especially, on a reasonable calculation, and on our own labours, we conceived that our provision and water, on a small allowance, would last us sixty days; that with the trade-wind, on the course we were then lying, we should be able to average the distance of a degree a day, which, in 26 days, would enable us to attain the region of the variable winds, and then, in thirty more, at the very utmost, should there be any favour in the elements, we might reach the coast.

With these considerations we commenced our voyage; the total failure of all which, and the subsequent dismal distress and suffering, by which we were overtaken, will be shown in the sequel. Our allowance of provision at first consisted of bread; one biscuit, weighing about one pound three ounces, and half a pint of water a day, for each man. This small quantity (less than one third which is required by an ordinary person), small as it was, we however took without murmuring, and, on many an occasion afterwards, blest God that even this pittance was allowed to us in our misery. The darkness of another night overtook us, and after having for the first time partook of our allowance of bread and water, we laid our weary bodies down in the boat, and endeavoured to get some repose.

Nature became at last worn out with the watchings and anxieties of the two preceding nights, and sleep came insensibly upon us. No dreams could break the strong fastenings of forgetfulness in which the mind was then locked up; but for my own part, my thoughts so haunted me that this luxury was yet a stranger to my eyes; every recollection was still fresh before me, and I enjoyed but a few short and unsatisfactory slumbers, caught in the intervals between my hopes and my fears. The dark ocean and swelling waters were nothing; the fears of being swallowed up by some dreadful tempest, or dashed upon hidden rocks, with all the other ordinary subjects of fearful contemplation, seemed scarcely entitled to a moment's thought; the dismal looking wreck, and the horrid aspect and revenge of the whale, wholly engrossed my reflections, until day again made its appearance.

November 23rd

In my chest, which I was fortunate enough to preserve, I had several small articles, which we found of great service to us; among the rest, some eight or ten sheets of writing paper, a lead pencil, a suit of clothes, three small fish hooks, a jack-knife, besides other useful purposes, served us as a razor. It was with much difficulty, however, that I could keep any sort of record, owing to the incessant rocking and unsteadiness of the boat, and the continual dashing of the spray of the sea over us.

The boat contained, in addition to the articles enumerated, a lantern, tinderbox, and two or three candles, which belonged to her, and with which they are kept always supplied, while engaged in taking whale. In addition to all which, the captain had saved a musket, two pistols, and a canister, containing about two pounds of gunpowder; the latter he distributed in equal proportions between the three boats, and gave the second mate and myself each a pistol.

When morning came we found ourselves quite near together, and the wind had considerably increased since the day before; we were consequently obliged to reef our sales and although we did not apprehend any very great danger from the then violence of the wind, yet it grew to be very uncomfortable in the boats, from the repeated dashing of the waves, that kept our bodies constantly wet with the salt spray. We, however, stood along our course until twelve o'clock, when we got an observation, as well as we were able to obtain one, while the water flew all over us, and the sea kept the boat extremely unsteady.

We found ourselves this day in latitude 0°58' S. having repassed the equator. We abandoned the idea altogether of keeping any correct longitudinal reckoning, having no glass, nor log-line. The wind moderated in the course of the afternoon a little, but at night came on to blow again almost a gale. We began now to tremble for our little barque; she was so ill calculated, in point of strength, to withstand the racking of the sea, while it required the constant labours of one man to keep her free of water.

We were surrounded in the afternoon with porpoises that kept playing about us in great numbers, and continued to follow us during the night.

November 24th

The wind had not abated any since the preceding day, and the sea had risen to be very large, and increased, if possible, the extreme uncomfortableness of our situation. What added more than anything else to our misfortunes, was, that all our efforts for the preservation of our provisions proved, in a great measure, ineffectual; a heavy sea broke suddenly into the boat, and before we could snatch it up, damaged some part of it; by timely attention, however, and great caution, we managed to make it eatable, and to preserve the rest from a similar casualty. This was a subject of extreme anxiety to us; the expectation, poor enough of itself indeed, upon which our final rescue was founded, must change at once to utter hopelessness, deprived of our provisions, the only means of continuing us in the exercise, not only of our manual powers, but in those of reason itself; hence, above all other things, this was the object of our utmost solicitude and pains.

We ascertained, the next day, that some of the provisions in the captain's boat had shared a similar fate during the night; both which accidents served to arouse us to a still stronger sense of our slender reliance upon the human means at our command, and to show us our utter dependence on that divine aid which we so much the more stood in need of.

November 25th

No change of wind had yet taken place, and we experienced the last night the same wet and disagreeable weather of the preceding one.

About eight o'clock in the morning we discovered that the water began to come fast in our boat, and in a few minutes the quantity increased to such a degree as to alarm us considerably for our safety; we commenced immediately a strict search in every part of her to discover the leak, and, after tearing up the ceiling or floor of the boat near the bows, we found it proceeded from one of the streaks or outside boards having bursted off there; no time was to be lost in devising some means to repair it.

The great difficulty consisted in its being in the bottom of the boat, and about six inches from the surface of the water; it was necessary, therefore, to have access to the outside, to enable us to fasten it on again: the leak being to leeward, we hove about, and lay to on the other tack which brought it then nearly out of water; the captain, who was at the time ahead of us, seeing us manoeuvring to get the boat about, shortened sail, and presently tacked, and ran down to us. I informed him of our situation, and he came immediately alongside to our assistance. After directing all the men in the boat to get on one side, the other, by that means, heeled out of the water a considerable distance, and, with a little difficulty, we then managed to drive in a few nails, and secured it, much beyond our expectations.

Fears of no ordinary kind were excited by this seemingly small accident. When it is recollected to what a slight vessel we had committed ourselves; our means of safety alone consisting in her capacity of endurance for many weeks, in all probability, yet to come, it will not be considered strange that this little accident should not only have damped our spirits considerably, but have thrown a great gloominess over the natural prospects of our deliverance. On this occasion, too, were we enabled to rescue ourselves from inevitable destruction by the possession of a few nails, without which (had it not been our fortune to save some from the wreck), we would, in all human calculation, have been lost: we were still liable to a recurrence of the same accident, perhaps to a still worse one, as, in the heavy and repeated racking of the swell, the progress of our voyage would serve but to increase the incapacity and weakness of our boat, and the starting of a single nail in her bottom would most assuredly prove our certain destruction. We wanted not this additional reflection, to add to the miseries of our situation.

November 26th

Our sufferings, heaven knows, were now sufficiently increased, and we looked forward, not without an extreme dread, and anxiety, to the gloomy and disheartening prospect before us.

We experienced a little abatement of wind and rough weather today, and took the opportunity of drying the bread that had been wet the day previously; to our great joy and satisfaction also, the wind hauled out to E.NE. and enabled us to hold a much more favourable course; with these exceptions, no circumstance of any considerable interest occurred in the course of this day.

The *27th of November* was alike undistinguished for any incident worthy of note; except that the wind again veered back to E. and destroyed the fine prospect we had entertained, of making a good run for several days to come.

November 28th

The wind hauled still further to the southward, and obliged us to fall off our course to S. and commenced to blow with such violence, as to put us again under short sail; the night set in extremely dark, and tempestuous, and we began to entertain fears that we should be separated. We however, with great pains, managed to keep about a ship's length apart, so that the white sails of our boats could be distinctly discernible. The captain's boat was but a short distance astern of mine, and that of the second mate a few rods to leeward of his.

At about 11 o'clock at night, having laid down to sleep, in the bottom of the boat. I was suddenly awakened by one of my companions, who cried out, that the captain was in distress, and was calling on us for assistance. I immediately aroused myself, and listened a moment, to hear if anything further should be said, when the captain's loud voice arrested my attention. He was calling to the second mate, whose boat was nearer to him than mine. I made all haste to put about, ran down to him, and inquired what was the matter; he replied, "I have been attacked by an unknown fish, and he has stove my boat."

It appeared that some large fish had accompanied the boat for a short distance, and had suddenly made an unprovoked attack upon her, as nearly as they could determine, with his jaws; the extreme darkness of the night prevented them from distinguishing what kind of animal it was, but they judged it to be about twelve feet in length, and one of the killer-fish species.

After having struck the boat once, he continued to play about her, on every side, as if manifesting a disposition to renew the attack, and did a second time strike the bows of the boat, and split her stem. They had no other instrument of offence, but the spirit-pole (a long slender piece of wood, by which the peak of the sail is extended), with which, after repeated attempts to destroy the boat, they succeeded in beating him off.

I arrived, just as he had discontinued his operations, and disappeared. He had made a considerable breach in the bows of the boat, through which the water had begun to pour fast; and the captain, imagining matters to be considerably worse than they were, immediately took measures to remove his provisions into the second mate's boat and mine, in order to lighten his own, and by that means, and constant bailing, to keep her above water until daylight should enable him to discover the extent of the damage, and to repair it.

The night was spissy darkness itself; the sky was completely overcast, and it seemed to us as if fate was wholly relentless, in pursuing us with such a cruel complication of disasters. We were not without our fears that the fish might renew his attack, some time during the night, upon one of the other boats, and unexpectedly destroy us; but they proved entirely groundless, as he was never afterwards seen.

When daylight came, the wind again favoured us a little, and we all lay to, to repair the broken; which was effected by nailing on this strips of boards in the inside; and having replaced the provisions, we proceeded again on our course.

Our allowance of water, which in the commencement, merely served to administer to the positive demands of nature, because now to insufficient; and we began to experience violent thirst, from the consumption of the provisions that had been wet with the salt water, and dried in the sun; of these we were obliged to eat first, to prevent their spoiling; and we could not, nay, we did not dare, to make any encroachments on our stock of water. Our determination was, to suffer as long as human patience and endurance would hold out, having only in view, the relief that would be afforded us, when the quantity of wet provisions should be exhausted.

Our extreme sufferings here first commenced. The privation of water is justly ranked among the most dreadful of the miseries of our life; the violence of raving thirst has no parallel in the catalogue of human calamities. It was our hard lot, to have felt this in its extremest force, when necessity subsequently compelled us to seek resource from one of the offices of nature. We were not, at first, aware of the consequences of eating this bread; and it was not until the fatal effects of it had shown themselves to a degree of oppression, that we could divine the cause of our extreme thirst.

But, alas! There was no relief. Ignorant, or instructed of the fact, it was alike immaterial; it composed a part of our subsistence, and reason imposed upon us the necessity of its immediate consumption, as otherwise it would have been lost to us entirely.

November 29th

Our boats appeared to be growing daily more frail and insufficient; the continual flowing of the water into them, seemed increased, without our being able to assign it to anything else, than a general weakness, arising from causes that must in a short time, without some remedy or relief, produce their total failure. We did not neglect, however, to patch up and mend them, according to our means, whenever we could discover a broken or weak part.

We this day found ourselves surrounded by a shoal of dolphins; some, or one of which, we tried in vain a long time to take. We made a small line from some rigging that was in the boat, fastened on one of the fish-hooks, and tied to it a small piece of white rag; they took not the least notice of it, but continued playing around us, nearly all day, mocking both our miseries and our efforts.

November 30th

This was a remarkably fine day; the weather not exceeded by any that we had experienced since we left the wreck. At one o'clock, I proposed to our boat's crew to kill one of the turtle; two of which we had in our possession. I need not say, that the proposition was hailed with the utmost enthusiasm; hunger had set its ravenous gnawings upon our stomachs, and we waited with impatience to suck the warm flowing blood of the animal.

A small fire was kindled in the shell of the turtle, and after dividing the blood (of which there was about a gill), among those of us who felt disposed to drink it, we cooked the remainder, entrails and all, and enjoyed from it an unspeakably fine repast. The stomachs of two or three revolted at the sight of the blood, and refused to partake of it; not even the outrageous thirst that was upon them could induce them to taste it; for myself, I took it like a medicine, to relieve the extreme dryness of my palate, and stopped not to inquire whether it was anything else than a liquid.

After this, I may say exquisite banquet, our bodies were considerably recruited, and I felt my spirits now much higher than they had been at any time before.

By observation, this day we found ourselves in latitude 7°53' S. our distance from the wreck, as nearly as we could calculate, was then about four hundred and eighty miles.

December 1st

From the 1st to the 3rd of December, exclusive, there was nothing transpired of any moment. Our boats as yet kept admirably well together, and the weather was distinguished for its mildness and salubrity. We gathered consolation too from a favourable slant which the wind took to NE, and our situation was not at that moment, we thought, so comfortless as we had been led at first to consider it; but, in our extravagant felicitations upon the blessing of the wind and weather, we forgot our leaks, our weak boats, our own debility, our immense distance from land, the smallness of our stock of provisions; all which, when brought to mind, with the force which they deserved, were too well calculated to dishearten us, and cause us to sigh for the hardships of our lot.

Up to the 3rd of December, the raging thirst of our mouths had not been but in a small degree alleviated; had it not been for the pains which that gave us, we should have tasted, during this spell of fine weather, a species of enjoyment, derived from a momentary forgetfulness of our actual situation.

December 3rd

With great joy we hailed the last crumb of our damaged bread, and commenced this day to take our allowance of healthy provisions. The salutary and agreeable effects of this change were felt at first in so slight a degree, as to give us no great cause of comfort or satisfaction; but gradually, as we partook of our small allowance of water, the moisture began to collect in our mouths, and the parching fever of the palate imperceptibly left it.

An accident here happened to us which gave us a great momentary spell of uneasiness. The night was dark, and the sky was completely overcast, so that we could scarcely discern each other's boats, when at about ten o'clock, that of the second mate was suddenly missing. I felt for a moment considerable alarm at her unexpected disappearance, but after a little reflection I immediately hove to, struck a light as expeditiously as possible, and hoisted it at the mast-head, in a lantern. Our eyes were now directed over every part of the ocean, in search of her, when, to our great joy, we discerned an answering light, about a quarter of a mile to leeward of us; we ran down to it, and it proved to be the lost boat.

Strange as the extraordinary interest which we felt in each other's company may appear, and much as our repugnance to separation may seem to imply of weakness, it was the subject of our continual hopes and fears. It is truly remarked, that misfortune more than anything else serves to endear us to our companions. So strongly was this sentiment engrafted upon our feelings, and so closely were the destinies of all of us involuntarily linked together, that, had one of the boats been wrecked, and wholly lost, with all her provisions and water, we should have felt ourselves constrained, by every tie of humanity, to have taken the surviving sufferers into the other boats, and shared our bread and water with them, while a crumb of one or a drop of the other remained. Hard, indeed, would the case have been for all, and much as I have since reflected on the subject, I have not been able to realize, had it so happened, that a sense of our necessities would have allowed us to give so magnanimous and devoted a character to our feelings. I can only speak of the impressions which I recollect I had at the time.

Subsequently, however as our situation became more straightened and desperate, our conversation on this subject took a different turn, and it appeared to be a universal sentiment, that such a course of conduct was calculated to weaken the chances of a final deliverance for some, and might be the only means of consigning every soul of us to a horrid death of starvation. There is no question but that an immediate separation, therefore, was the most politic measure that could be adopted, and that every boat should take its own separate chance: while we remained together, should any accident happen, of the nature alluded to, no other course could be adopted, than that of taking the survivors into the other boats, and giving up voluntarily, what we were satisfied could alone prolong our hopes, and multiply the chances of our safety, or unconcernedly witness their struggles in death, perhaps beat them from our boats, with weapons, back into the ocean.

The expectation of reaching the land was founded upon a reasonable calculation of the distance, the means, and the subsistence; all which were scanty enough. God knows, and ill adapted to the probable exigencies of the voyage. Any addition to our own demands, in this respect, would not only injure, but actually destroy the whole system which we had laid down, and reduce us to a slight hope, derived either from the speedy death of some of our crew, or the falling in with some vessel.

With all this, however, there was a desperate instinct that bound us together; we could not reason on the subject with any degree of satisfaction to our minds, yet we continued to cling to each other with a strong and involuntary impulse. This, indeed, was a matter of no small difficulty, and it constituted, more than anything else, a source of continual watching and inquietude. We would but turn our eyes away for a few moments, during some dark nights, and presently, one of the boats would be missing. There was no other remedy than to heave to immediately and set a light, by which the missing boat might be directed to us. These proceedings necessarily interfered very much with our speed, and consequently lessened our hopes, but we preferred to submit to it, while the consequences were not so immediately felt, rather than part with the consolation which each other's presence afforded.

Nothing of importance took place on the 4th of December; and on the 5th, at night, owing to the extreme darkness, and a strong wind, I again separated from the other boats. Finding they were not to be seen in any direction, I loaded my pistol and fired it twice; soon after the second discharge they made their appearance a short distance to windward, and we joined company, and again kept on our course, in which we continued without any remarkable occurrence, through the 6th and 7th of December. The wind during this period blew very strong, and much more unfavourably. Our boats continued to leak, and to take in a good deal of water over the gunwales.

December 8th

In the afternoon of this day the wind set in E.SE. and began to blow much harder than we had yet experienced it; by twelve o'clock at night it had increased to a perfect gale, with heavy showers of rain, and we now began, from these dreadful indications, to prepare ourselves for destruction. We continued to take in sail by degrees, as the tempest gradually increased, until at last we were obliged to take down our masts. At this juncture we gave up entirely to the mercy of the waves.

The sea and rain had wet us to the skin, and we sat down, silently, and with sullen resignation, awaited our fate. We made an effort to catch some fresh water by spreading one of the sails, but after having spent a long time, and obtained but a small quantity in a bucket, it proved to be quite as salt as that from the ocean: this we attributed to its having passed through the sail which had been so often wet by the sea, and upon which, after drying so frequently in the sun, concretions of salt had been formed.

It was a dreadful night – cut off from any imaginary relief – nothing remained but to await the approaching issue with firmness and resignation. The appearance of the heavens was dark and dreary, and the blackness that was spread over the face of the waters dismal beyond description. The heavy squalls, that followed each other in quick succession, were preceded by sharp flashes of lightning, that appeared to wrap our little barge in flames. The sea rose to a fearful height, and every wave that came looked as if it must be the last that would be necessary for our destruction. To an overruling Providence alone must be attributed our salvation from the horrors of that terrible night. It can be accounted for in no other way: that a speck of substance, like that which we were, before the driving terrors of the tempest, could have been conducted safely through it.

At twelve o'clock it began to abate a little in intervals of two or three minutes, during which we would venture to raise up our heads and look to windward. Our boat was completely unmanageable; without sails, mast, or rudder, and had been driven, in the course of the afternoon and night, we knew no whither, nor how far. When the gale had in some measure subsided we made efforts to get a little sail upon her, and put her head towards the course we had been steering. My companions had not slept any during the whole night and were dispirited and broken down to such a degree as to appear to want some more powerful stimulus than the fears of death to enable them to do their duty. By great exertions, however, towards morning we again set a double-reefed mainsail and jib upon her, and began to make tolerable progress on the voyage. An unaccountable good fortune had kept the boats together during all the troubles of the night: and the sun rose and showed the disconsolate faces of our companions once more to each other.

December 9th

By twelve o'clock this day we were enabled to set all sail as usual; but there continued to be a very heavy sea running, which opened the seams of the boats, and increased the leaks to an alarming degree. There was, however, no remedy for this but continual bailing, which had now become to be an extremely irksome and laborious task. By observation we found ourselves in latitude 17°40' S.

At eleven o'clock at night, the captain's boat was unexpectedly found to be missing. After the last accident of this kind we had agreed, if the same should again occur, that, in order to save our time, the other boats should not heave to, as usual, but continue on their course until morning, and thereby save the great detention that must arise from such repeated delays. We, however, concluded on this occasion to make a small effort, which, if it did not immediately prove the means of restoring the lost boat, we would discontinue, and again make sail. Accordingly we hove to for an hour, during which time I fired my pistol twice, and obtaining no tidings of the boat, we stood on our course. When daylight appeared she was to leeward of us, about two miles; upon observing her we immediately ran down, and again joined company.

December 10th

I have omitted to notice the gradual advances which hunger and thirst, for the last six days, had made upon us. As the time had lengthened since our departure from the wreck, and the allowance of provision, making the demands of the appetite daily more and more importunate, they had created in us an almost uncontrollable temptation to violate our resolution, and satisfy, for once, the hard yearnings of nature from our stock; but a little reflection served to convince us of the imprudence and unmanliness of the measure, and it was abandoned with a sort of melancholy effort of satisfaction.

I had taken into custody, by common consent, all the provisions and water belonging to the boat, and was determined that no encroachments should be made upon it with my consent; nay, I felt myself bound, by every consideration of duty, by every dictate of sense, of prudence, and discretion, without which, in my situation, all other exertions would have been folly itself, to protect them, at the hazard of my life. For this purpose, I locked up in my chest the whole quantity, and never, for a single moment, closed my eyes without placing some part of my person in contact with the chest; and having loaded my pistol, kept it constantly about me.

I should not certainly have put any threats in execution as long as the most distant hopes of reconciliation existed; and was determined, in case the least refractory disposition should be manifested (a thing which I contemplated not unlikely to happen, with a set of starving wretches like ourselves), that I would immediately divide our subsistence into equal proportions, and give each man's share into his own keeping. Then, should any attempt be made upon mind, which I intended to mete out to myself, according to exigencies, I was resolved to make the consequences of it fatal.

There was, however, the most upright and obedient behavior in this respect manifested by every man in the boat, and I never had the least opportunity of proving what my conduct would have been on such an occasion. While standing on our course this day we came across a small shoal of flying fish: four of which, in their efforts to avoid us, flew against the mainsail, and dropped into the boat; one, having fell near me, I eagerly snatched up and devoured; the other three were immediately taken by the rest, and eaten alive. For the first time I, on this occasion, felt a disposition to laugh, upon witnessing the ludicrous and almost desperate efforts of my five companions, who each sought to get a fish. They were very small of the kind, and constituted but an extremely delicate mouthful, scales, wings, and all for hungry stomachs like ours.

From the eleventh to the thirteenth of December inclusive, our progress was very slow, owing to light winds and calms; and nothing transpired of any moment, except that on the eleventh we killed the only remaining turtle, and enjoyed another luxuriant repast, that invigorated our bodies, and gave a fresh flow to our spirits.

The weather was extremely hot, and we were exposed to the full force of a meridian sun, without any covering to shield us from its burning influence, or the least breath of air to cool its parched rays.

On the thirteenth day of December we were blessed with a change of wind to the northward, that brought us a most welcome and unlooked for relief. We now, for the first time, actually felt what might be deemed a reasonable hope of our deliverance; and with hearts bounding with satisfaction, and bosoms swelling with joy, we made all sail to the eastward. We imagined we had run out of the trade-winds, and had got into the variables, and should, in all probability, reach the land many days sooner than we expected. But, alas! Our anticipations were but a dream, from which we shortly experienced a cruel awakening.

The wind gradually died away, and at night was succeeded by a perfect calm, more oppressive and disheartening to us, from the bright prospects which had attended us during the day. The gloomy reflections that this hard fortune had given birth to, were succeeded by others, of a no less cruel and discouraging nature, when we found the calm continue during the fourteenth, fifteenth, and sixteenth of December inclusive. The extreme oppression of the weather, the sudden and unexpected prostration of our hopes, and the consequent dejection of our spirits, set us again to thinking, and filled our souls with fearful and melancholy forebodings. In this state of affairs, seeing no alternative left us but to employ to the best advantage all human expedients in our power, I proposed, on the fourteenth, to reduce our allowance of provisions one half.

No objections were made to this arrangement: all submitted, or seemed to do so, with an admirable fortitude and forbearance. The proportion which our stock of water bore to our bread was not large; and while the weather continued so oppressive, we did not think it advisable to diminish our scanty pittance; indeed, it would have been scarcely possible to have done so, with any regard to our necessities, as our thirst had become now incessantly more intolerable than hunger, and the quantity then allowed was barely sufficient to keep the mouth in a state of moisture, for about one-third of the time.

"Patience and long-suffering" was the constant language of our lips: and a determination, strong as the resolves of the soul could make it, to cling to existence as long as hope and breath remained in us. In vain was every expedient tried to relieve the raging fever of the throat by drinking salt water, and holding small quantities of it in the mouth, until, by that means, the thirst was increased to such a degree, as even to drive us to despairing, and vain relief from our own urine. Our sufferings during these calm days almost succeeded human belief. The hot rays of the sun beat down upon us to such a degree, as to oblige us to hang over the gunwale of the boat, into the sea, to cool our weak and fainting bodies. This expedient afforded us, however, a grateful relief, and was productive of a discovery of infinite importance to us. No sooner had one of us got on the outside of the gunwale than he immediately observed the bottom of the boat to be covered with a species of small clam, which, upon being tasted, proved a most delicious and agreeable food.

This was no sooner announced to us, than we commenced to tear them off and eat them, for a few minutes, like a set of gluttons; and, after having satisfied the immediate craving of the stomach, we gathered large quantities and laid them up in the boat; but hunger came upon us again in less than half an hour afterwards within which time they had all disappeared.

Upon attempting to get in again, we found ourselves so weak as to require each other's assistance; indeed, had it not been for three of our crew, who could not swim, and who did not, therefore, get overboard, I know not by what means we should have been able to have resumed our situations in the boat.

On the fifteenth our boat continued to take in water so fast from her leaks, and the weather proving so moderate, we concluded to search out the bad places, and endeavour to mend them as well as we should be able. After a considerable search, and, removing the ceiling near the bows, we found the principal opening was occasioned by the starting of a plank or strake in the bottom of the boat, next to the keel. To remedy this, it was now absolutely necessary to have access to the bottom. The means of doing which did not immediately occur in our minds. After a moment's reflection, however, one of the crew, Benjamin Lawrence, offered to tie a rope around his body, take a boat's hatchet in his hand, and thus go under the water, and hold the hatchet against a nail, to be driven through from the inside, for the purpose of clenching it. This was, accordingly, all effected, with some little trouble, and answered the purpose much beyond our expectations.

Our latitude was this day 21°42' South. The oppression of our weather still continuing through the sixteenth, bore upon our health and spirits with an amazing force and severity. The most disagreeable excitements were produced by it, which, added to the disconsolate endurance of the calm, called loudly for some mitigating expedient – some sort of relief to our prolonged sufferings.

By our observations today we found, in addition to our other calamities, that we had been urged back from our progress, by the heave of the sea, a distance of ten miles; and were still without any prospect of wind. In this distressing posture of our affairs, the captain proposed that we should commence rowing, which, being seconded by all, we immediately concluded to take a double allowance of provision and water for a day, and row, during the cool of the nights, until we should get a breeze from some quarter or other.

Accordingly, when night came, we commenced our laborious operations: we made but a very sorry progress. Hunger and thirst, and long inactivity, had so weakened us, that in three hours every man gave out, and we abandoned the further prosecution of the plan.

With the sunrise the next morning, on the seventeenth, a light breeze sprung up from the SE. and, although directly ahead, it was welcomed with almost frenzied feelings of gratitude and joy.

December 18th

The wind had increased this day considerably, and by twelve o'clock blew a gale; veering from SE. to E.SE. Again we were compelled to take in all sail, and lie to for the principal part of the day. At night, however, it died away, and the next day, the nineteenth, proved very moderate and pleasant weather, and we again commenced to make a little progress.

December 20th

This was a day of great happiness and joy. After having experienced one of the most distressing nights in the whole catalogue of our sufferings, we awoke to a morning of comparative luxury and pleasure. About 7 o'clock, while we were sitting dispirited, silent, and dejected, in our boats, one of our companions suddenly and loudly called out, "There is land!"

We were all aroused in an instant, as if electrified, and casting our eyes to leeward, there indeed, was the blessed vision before us, as plain and palpable as could be wished for.

A new and extraordinary impulse now took possession of us. We shook off the lethargy of our senses, and seemed to take another, and a fresh existence. One or two of my companions, whose lagging spirits, and worn out frames, had begun to inspire them with an utter indifference to their fate, now immediately brightened up, and manifested a surprising alacrity and earnestness to gain, without delay, the much wished for shore. It appeared at first a low, white beach, and lay like a basking paradise before our longing eyes. It was discovered nearly at the same time by the other boats, and a general burst of joy and congratulation now passed between us.

It is not within the scope of human calculation, by a mere listener to the story, to divine what the feelings of our hearts were on this occasion. Alternate expectation, fear, gratitude, surprise, and exultation, each swayed our minds, and quickened our exertions. We ran down for it, and at 11 o'clock a.m. we were within a quarter of a mile of the shore.

It was an island, to all appearance, as nearly as we could determine it, about six miles long, and three broad; with a very high, rugged shore, and surrounded by rocks; the sides of the mountains were bare, but on the tops it looked fresh and green with vegetation. Upon examining our navigators, we found it was Ducie's Island, lying in latitude 24°40' S. longitude 124°40' W. 14.

A short moment sufficed for reflection, and we made immediate arrangements to land. None of us knew whether the island was inhabited or not, nor what it afforded, if anything; if inhabited, it was uncertain whether by beasts or savages; and a momentary suspense was created, by the dangers which might possibly arise by proceeding without due preparation and care.

Hunger and thirst, however, soon determined us, and having taken the musket and pistols, I, with three others, effected a landing upon some sunken rocks, and waded thence to the shore.

Upon arriving at the beach, it was necessary to take a little breath, and we laid down for a few minutes to rest our weak bodies, before we could proceed. Let the reader judge, if he can, what must have been our feelings now! Bereft of all comfortable hopes of life, for the space of thirty days of terrible suffering; our bodies wasted to mere skeletons, by hunger and thirst, and death itself staring us in the face; to be suddenly and unexpectedly conducted to a rich banquet of food and drink, which subsequently we enjoyed for a few days, to our full satisfaction; and he will have but a faint idea of the happiness that here fell to our lot.

We now, after a few minutes, separated, and went different directions in search of water; the want of which had been our principal privation, and called for immediate relief. I had not proceeded far in my excursion, before I discovered a fish, about a foot and a half in length, swimming along in the water close to the shore. I commenced an attack upon him with the breach of my gun, and struck him, I believe, once, and he ran under a small rock, that lay near the shore, from whence I took him with the aid of my ramrod, and brought him up on the beach, and immediately fell to eating. My companions soon joined in the repast; and in less than ten minutes the whole was consumed, bones, and skin, and scales, and all. With full stomachs, we imagined we could now attempt the mountains, where, if in any part of the island, we considered water would be most probably obtained.

I accordingly clambered, with excessive labour, suffering, and pain, up amongst the bushes, roots, and underwood, of one of the crags, looking in all directions in vain, for every appearance of water that might present itself. There was no indication of the least moisture to be found, within the distance to which I had ascended, although my strength did not enable me to get higher than about 20 feet.

I was sitting down at the height that I had attained, to gather a little breath, and ruminating upon the fruitlessness of my search, and the consequent evils and continuation of suffering that is necessarily implied, when I perceived that the tide had risen considerably since our landing, and threatened to cut off our retreat to the rocks, by which alone we should be able to regain our boats. I therefore determined to proceed again to the shore, and inform the captain and the rest of our want of success in procuring water, and consult upon the propriety of remaining at the island any longer.

I never for one moment lost sight of the main chance, which I conceived we still had, of either getting to the coast, or of meeting with some vessel at sea; and felt that every minute's detention, without some equivalent object, was lessening those chances, by a consumption of the means of our support.

When I had got down, one of my companions informed me, that he had found a place in a rock some distance off, from which the water exuded in small drops, at intervals of about five minutes, that he had, by applying his lips to the rock, obtained a few of them, which only served to whet his appetite, and from which nothing like the least satisfaction had proceeded. I immediately resolved in my own mind, upon this information, to advise remaining until morning, to endeavour to make a more thorough search the next day, and with our hatchets to pick away the rock which had been discovered, with the view of increasing, if possible, the run of the water.

We all repaired again to our boats, and there found that the captain had the same impressions as to the propriety of our delay until morning. We therefore landed; and having hauled our boats up on the beach, laid down in them that night, free from all the anxieties of watching and labour, and amid all our sufferings, gave ourselves up to an unreserved forgetfulness and peace of mind, that seemed so well to accord with the pleasing anticipations that this day had brought forth.

It was but a short space, however, until the morning broke upon us; and sense, and feeling, and gnawing hunger, and the raging fever of thirst then redoubled my wishes and efforts to explore the island again.

We had obtained, that night, a few crabs, by traversing the shore a considerable distance, and a few very small fish; but waited until the next day, for the labours of which, we considered a night of refreshing and undisturbed repose would better qualify us.

December 21st

We had still reserved our common allowance, but it was entirely inadequate for the purpose of supplying the raging demand of the palate, and such an excessive and cruel thirst was created, as almost to deprive us of the power of speech. The lips became cracked and swollen, and a sort of glutinous saliva collected in the mouth, disagreeable to the taste, and intolerable beyond expression. Our bodies had wasted away to almost skin and bone, and possessed so little strength, as often to require each other's assistance in performing some of its weakest functions. Relief, we now felt, must come soon, or nature would sink.

The most perfect discipline was still maintained, in respect to our provisions; and it now became our whole object, if we should not be able to replenish our subsistence from the island, to obtain, by some means or other, a sufficient refreshment to enable us to prosecute our voyage.

Our search for water accordingly again commenced with the morning; each of us took a different direction, and prosecuted the examination of every place where there was the least indication of it; the small leaves of the shrubbery, affording a temporary alleviation, by being chewed in the mouth, and but for the peculiarly bitter taste which those of the island possessed, would have been an extremely grateful substitute.

In the course of our rambles too, along the sides of the mountain, we would now and then meet with tropic birds, of a beautiful figure and plumage occupying small holes in the sides of it, from which we plucked them without the least difficulty. Upon our approaching them they made no attempts to fly, nor did they appear to notice us at all. These birds served us for a fine repast; numbers of which were caught in the course of the day, cooked by fires which we made on the shore, and eaten with the utmost avidity.

We found also a plant, in taste not unlike the peppergrass, growing in considerable abundance in the crevices of the rocks, and which proved to us a very agreeable food, by being chewed with the meat of the birds.

These, with birds' nests, some of them full of young, and others of eggs, a few of which we found in the course of the day, served us for food, and supplied the place of our bread; from the use of which, during our stay here, we had restricted ourselves. But water, the great object of all our anxieties and exertions, was nowhere to be found, and we began to despair of meeting with it on the island.

Our state of extreme weakness, and many of us without shoes or any covering for the feet, prevented us from exploring any great distance, lest by some sudden faintness, or over exertion, we should not be able to return, and at night be exposed to attacks of wild beasts, which might inhabit the island, and be alike incapable of resistance, as beyond the reach of the feeble assistance that otherwise could be afforded to each. The whole day was thus consumed in picking up whatever had the least shape or quality of sustenance, and another night of misery was before us, to be passed without a drop of water to cool our parching tongues.

In this state of affairs, we could not reconcile it to ourselves to remain longer at this place; a day, and hour, lost to us unnecessarily here, might cost us our preservation. A drop of the water that we then had in our possession might prove, in the last stages of our debility, the very cordial of life. I addressed the substance of these few reflections to the captain, who agreed with me in opinion, upon the necessity of taking some decisive steps in our present dilemma.

After some considerable conversation on this subject, it was finally concluded, to spend the succeeding day in the further search for water, and if none should be found, to quit the island the morning after.

December 23rd

We had been employed during the last night to various occupations, according to the feelings or the wants of the men; some continued to wander about the shore, and to short distances in the mountains, still seeking for food and water; others hung about the beach, near the edge of the sea, endeavouring to take the little fish that came about them. Some slept, insensible to every feeling but rest; while others spent the night in talking of their situation, and reasoning upon the probabilities of their deliverance.

The dawn of day aroused us again to labour, and each of us pursued his own inclination, as the course taken over the island after water. My principal hope was founded upon my success in picking the rocks where the moisture had been discovered the day before, the thither I hastened as soon as my strength would enable me to get there.

It was about a quarter of a mile from what I may call our encampment; and with two men, who had accompanied me. I commenced my labours with a hatchet and an old chisel. The rock proved to be very soft, and in a very short time I had obtained a considerable hole, but, alas! Without the least wished-for effect. I watched it for some little time with great anxiety, hoping that, as I increased the depth of the hole, the water would presently flow; but all my hopes and efforts were unavailing, and at last I desisted from further labour, and sat down near it in utter despair.

As I turned my eyes towards the beach I saw some of the men in the act of carrying a keg along from the boats, with, I thought, an extraordinary spirit and activity; and the idea suddenly darted across my mind that they had found water, and were taking a keg to fill it. I quitted my seat in a moment, made the best of my way towards them, with a palpitating heart, and before I came up with them, they gave me the cheering news that they had found a spring of water.

I felt, at that moment, as if I could have fallen down and thanked God for this signal act of his mercy. The sensation that I experienced was indeed strange, and such as I shall never forget. At one instant I felt an almost choking excess of joy, and at the next I wanted the relief of a flood of tears.

When I arrived at the spot, whither I had hastened as fast as my weak legs would carry me, I found my companions had all taken their fill, and with an extreme degree of forbearance I then satisfied myself, by drinking in small quantities, and at intervals of two or three minutes apart. Many had, notwithstanding the remonstrances of prudence, and, in some cases, force, laid down and thoughtlessly swallowed large quantities of it, until they could drink no more. The effect of this was, however, neither so sudden nor bad as we had imagined; it only served to make them a little stupid and indolent for the remainder of the day.

Upon examining the place from whence we had obtained this miraculous and unexpected succour, we were equally astonished and delighted with the discovery. It was on the shore, above which the sea flowed to the depth of near six feet; and we could procure the water, therefore, from it only when the tide was down. The crevice from which it rose was in a flat rock, large surfaces of which were spread around, and composed the face of the beach.

We filled our two kegs before the tide rose, and went back again to our boats. The remainder of this day was spent in seeking for fish, crabs, birds, and anything else that fell in our way, that could contribute to satisfy our appetites; and we enjoyed, during that night, a most comfortable and delicious sleep, unattended with those violent cravings of hunger and thirst, that had poisoned our slumbers for so many previous ones.

Since the discovery of the water, too, we began to entertain different notions altogether of our situation. There was no doubt we might here depend upon a constant and ample supply of it as long as we chose to remain, and, in all probability, we could manage to obtain food, until the island should be visited by some vessel, or time allowed to devise other means of leaving it. Our boats would still remain to us: a stay here might enable us to mend, straighten, and put them in more perfect order for the sea, and get ourselves so far recruited as to be able to endure, if necessary, a more protracted voyage to the main land.

I made a silent determination in my own mind that I would myself pursue something like this plan, whatever might be the opinion of the rest; but I found no difference in the views of any of us as to this matter. We, therefore, concluded to remain at least four or five days, within which time it could be sufficiently known whether it would be advisable to make any arrangement for a more permanent abode.

At 11 o'clock a.m. we again visited our spring: the tide had fallen to about a foot below it, and we were able to procure, before it rose again, about twenty gallons of water. It was at first a little brackish, but soon became fresh, from the constant supply from the rock, and the departure of the sea. Our observations this morning tended to give us every confidence in its quantity and quality, and we, therefore, rested perfectly easy in our minds on the subject, and commenced to make further discoveries about the island.

Each man sought for his own daily living, on whatsoever the mountains, the shore, or the sea, could furnish him with; and every day, during our stay there, the whole time was employed in roving about for food.

We found, however, on the twenty-fourth, that we had picked up, on the island, everything that could be got at, in the way of sustenance; and, much to our surprise, some of the men came in at night and complained of not having gotten sufficient during the day to satisfy the cravings of their stomachs.

Every accessible part of the mountain, contiguous to us, or within the reach of our weak enterprise, was already ransacked, for birds' eggs and grass, and was rifled of all that they contained: so that we began to entertain serious apprehensions that we should not be able to live long here; at any rate, with the view of being prepared, as well as possible, should necessity at any time oblige us to quit it, we commenced, on the twenty-fourth, to repair our boats, and continued to work upon them all that and the succeeding day. We were enabled to do this, with much facility, by drawing them up and turning them over on the beach, working by spells of two or three hours at a time, and then leaving off to seek for food. We procured our water daily, when the tide would leave the shore: but on the evening of the twenty-fifth, found that a fruitless search for nourishment had not repaid us for the labours of a whole day.

There was no one thing on the island upon which we could in the lest degree rely, except the peppergrass, and of that the supply was precarious, and not much relished without some other food. Our situation here, therefore, now became worse than it would have been in our boats on the ocean; because, in the latter case, we should be still making some progress towards the land, while our provisions lasted, and the chance of falling in with some vessel be considerably increased. It was certain that we ought not to remain here unless upon the strongest assurances in our own minds, of sufficient sustenance, and that, too, in regular supplies, that might be depended upon.

After much conversation amongst us on this subject, and again examining our navigators, it was finally concluded to set sail for Easter Island, which we found to be E.SE. from us in latitude 27°9' S. longitude 109°35' W. All we knew of this island was, that it existed as laid down in the books; but of its extent, productions, or inhabitants, if any, we were entirely ignorant; at any rate, it was nearer by eighty hundred and fifty miles to the coast, and could not be worse in its productions than the one we were about leaving.

The twenty-sixth of December was wholly employed in preparations for our departure; our boats were hauled down to the vicinity of the spring and our casks, and everything else that would contain it, filled with water.

There had been considerable talk between three of our companions, about their remaining on this island, and taking their chance both for a living, and an escape from it; and as the time drew near at which we were to leave, they made up their minds to stay behind. The rest of us could make no objection to their plan, as it lessened the load of our boats, allowed us their share of the provisions, and the probability of their being able to sustain themselves on the island was much stronger than that of our reaching the main land. Should we, however, ever arrive safely, it would become our duty, and we so assured them, to give information of their situation, and make every effort to procure their removal from thence; which we accordingly afterwards did.

Their names were William Wright of Barnstable, Massachusetts, Thomas Chapple of Plymouth, England, and Seth Weeks of the former place. They had begun, before we came away, to construct a sort of habitation, composed of the branches of trees, and we left with them every article that could be spared from the boats. It was their intention to build a considerable dwelling, that could protect them from the rains, as soon as time and materials could be provided. The captain wrote letters, to be left on the island, giving information of the fate of the ship, and that of our own; and stating that we had set out to reach Easter Island, with further particulars, intended to give notice (should our fellow-sufferers die there, and the place be ever visited by any vessel) of our misfortunes. These letters were put in a tin case, enclosed in a small wooden box, and nailed to a tree, on the west side of the island, near our landing place. We had observed, some days previously, the name of a ship, "The Elizabeth", cut out in the bark of this tree, which rendered it indubitable that one of that name had once touched here. There was, however, no date to it, or anything else, by which any further particulars could be made out.

December 27th

I went, before we set sail this morning, and procured for each boat a flat stone, and two arms-full of wood, with which to make a fire in our boats, should it become afterwards necessary in the further prosecution of our voyage; as we calculated we might catch a fish, or a bird, and in that case be provided with the means of cooking it; otherwise, from the intense heat of weather, we knew they could not be preserved from spoiling.

At ten o'clock a.m. the tide having risen far enough to allow our boats to float over the rocks, we made all sail, and steered around the island, for the purpose of making a little further observation, which would not detail us any time, and might be productive of some unexpected good fortune. Before we started we missed our three companions, and found they had not come down, either to assist us to get off, nor to take any kind of leave of us.

I walked up the beach towards their rude dwelling, and informed them that we were then about to set sail, and should probably never see them more. They seemed to be very much affected, and one of them shed tears. They wished us to write to their relations, should Providence safely direct us again to our homes, and said but little else. They had every confidence in being able to procure a subsistence there as long as they remained: and, finding them ill at heart about taking any leave of us, I hastily bid them "good-bye," hoped they would do well, and came away. They followed me with their eyes until I was out of sight, and I never saw more of them.

On the NW side of the island we perceived a fine white beach, on which we imagined we might land, and in a short time ascertain if any further useful discoveries could be effected, or any addition made to our stock of provisions; and having set ashore five or six of the men for this purpose, the rest of us shoved off the boats and commenced fishing. We saw a number of sharks, but all efforts to take them proved ineffectual; and we got but a few small fish, about the size of a mackerel, which we divided amongst us. In this business we were occupied for the remainder of the day, until six o'clock in the afternoon, when the men, having returned to the shore from their search in the mountains, brought a few birds, and we again set sail and steered directly for Easter Island.

During that night, after we had got quite clear of the land, we had a fine strong breeze from the NW.; we kept our fires going, and cooked our fish and birds, and felt our situation as comfortable as could be expected. We continued on our course, consuming our provisions and water as sparingly as possible, without any material incident, until the thirtieth, when the wind hauled out E.SE. directly ahead, and so continued until the thirty-first, when it again came to the northward, and we resumed our course.

On the third of January we experienced heavy squalls from the W.SW. accompanied with dreadful thunder and lightning, that threw a gloomy and cheerless aspect over the ocean, and incited a recurrence of some of those heavy and desponding moments that we had before experienced.

We commenced from Ducies Island to keep a regular reckoning, by which, on the fourth of January, we found we had got to the southward of Easter Island, and the wind prevaiing E.NE. we should not be able to get on the eastward, so as to reach it.

Our birds and fish were all now consumed, and we had begun again upon our short allowance of bread. It was necessary, in this state of things, to change our determination of going to Easter Island, and shape our course in some other direction, where the wind would allow of our going. We had but little hesitation in concluding, therefore, to steer for the island of Juan Fernandez, which lay about E.SE. from us, distant two thousand five hundred miles. We bent our course accordingly towards it, having for the two succeeding days very light winds, and suffering excessively from the intense heat of the sun. The seventh brought us a change of wind in the northward, and at twelve o'clock we found ourselves in latitude 30°18' S. longitude 117°29' W. We continued to make what progress we could to the eastward.

January 10th

Matthew P. Joy, the second mate, had suffered from debility, and the privations we had experienced, much beyond any of the rest of us, and was on the eighth removed to the captain's boat, under the impression that he would be more comfortable there, and more attention and pains be bestowed in nursing and endeavouring to comfort him. This day being calm, he manifested a desire to be taken back again; but at 4 o'clock in the afternoon, after having been, according to his wishes, placed in his own boat, he died very suddenly after his removal.

On the eleventh, at six o'clock in the morning, we sewed him up in his clothes, tied a large stone to his feet, and having brought all the boats to, consigned him in a solemn manner to the ocean. This man did not die of absolute starvation, although his end was no doubt very much hastened by his sufferings. He had a weak and sickly constitution, and complained of being unwell the whole voyage. It was an incident, however, which threw a gloom over our feelings for many days.

In consequence of his death, one man from the captain's boat was placed in that from which he died to supply his place, and we stood away again from our course.

On the 12th of January we had the wind from the NW., which commenced in the morning, and came on to blow before night a perfect gale. We were obliged to take in all sail and run before the wind. Flashes of lightning were quick and vivid, and the rain came down in cataracts. As however that gale blew us fairly on our course, and our speed being great during the day, we derived, I may say, even pleasure from the uncomfortableness and fury of the storm.

We were apprehensive that in the darkness of this night we should be separated, and made arrangements, each boat to keep an E.SE course all night. About eleven o'clock my boat being ahead a short distance of the others, I turned my head back, as I was in the habit of doing every minute, and neither of the others were to be seen. It was blowing and raining at this time as if the heavens were separating, and I knew not hardly at the moment what to do. I hove my boat to the wind, and lay drifting about an hours, expecting every moment that they would come up with me, but not seeing anything of them, I put away again, and stood on the course agreed upon, with strong hopes that daylight would enable me to discover them again.

When the morning dawned, in vain did we look over every part of the ocean for our companions; they were gone! And we saw no more of them afterwards. It was folly to repine at the circumstances; it could neither be remedied, nor could sorrow secure their return; but it was impossible to prevent ourselves feeling all poignancy and bitterness that characterizes the separation of men who have long suffered in each other's company, and whose interests and feelings fate had so closely linked together.

By our observation, we separated in latitude 32°16' S. longitude 112°20' W. 11. For many days after this accident, our progress was attended with dull and melancholy reflections. We had lost the cheering of each other's faces, that, which strange as it is, we so much required in both our mental and bodily distresses.

The 14th of January proved another very squally and rainy day. We had now been nineteen days from the island, and had made a distance of about 900 miles: necessity began to whisper us, that a still further reduction of our allowance must take place, or we must abandon altogether the hopes of reaching the land, and rely wholly on the chance of being taken up by a vessel. But how to reduce the daily quantity of food, with any regard to life itself, was a question of the utmost consequence.

Upon our first leaving the wreck, the demands of the stomach had been circumscribed to the smallest possible compass; and subsequently before reaching the island, a diminution had taken place of nearly one-half; and it was now, from a reasonable calculation, become necessary even to curtail that at least one-half; which must, in a short time, reduce us to mere skeletons again.

We had a full allowance of water, but it only served to contribute to our debility; our bodies deriving but the scanty support which an ounce and a half of bread for each man afforded. It required a great effort to bring matters to this dreadful alternative, either to feed our bodies and our hopes a little longer, or in the agonies of hunger to seize upon and devour our provisions, and coolly await the approach of death.

We were as yet, just able to move about in our boats, and slowly perform the necessary labours appertaining to her; but we were fast wasting away with the relaxing effects of the water, and we daily almost perished under the torrid rays of a meridian sun; to escape which, we would lie down in the bottom of the boat, cover ourselves over with the sails, and abandon her to the mercy of the waves. Upon attempting to rise again, the blood would rush into the head, and an intoxicating blindness come over us, almost to occasion our suddenly falling down again. A slight interest was still kept up in our minds by the distant hopes of yet meeting with the other boats, but it was never realized.

An accident occurred at night, which gave me a great cause of uneasiness, and led me to an unpleasant rumination upon the probable consequences of a repetition of it. I had laid down in the boat without taking the usual precaution of securing the lid of the provision-chest, as I was accustomed to do, when one of the white men awoke me, and informed me that one of the blacks had taken some bread from it. I felt at the moment the highest indignation and resentment at such conduct in any of our crew, and immediately took my pistol in my hand, and charged him if he had taken any, to give it up without the least hesitation, or I should instantly shoot him! –

He became at once very much alarmed, and, trembling, confessed the fact, pleading the hard necessity that urged him to it: he appeared to be very penitent for his crime, and earnestly swore that he would never be guilty of it again. I could not find it in my soul to extend towards him the least severity on this account, however much, according to the strict imposition which we felt upon ourselves it might demand it.

This was the first infraction; and the security of our lives, our hopes of redemption from our sufferings, loudly called for a prompt and signal punishment; but every humane feeling of nature plead in his behalf, and he was permitted to escape, with the solemn injunction, that a repetition of the same offence would cost him his life.

I had almost determined upon this occurrence to divide our provisions, and give to each man his share of the whole stock; and should have done so in the height of my resentment, had it not been for the reflection that some might, by imprudence, be tempted to go beyond the daily allowance, or consume it all at once, and bring on a premature weakness or starvation: this would of course disable them for the duties of the boat, and reduce our chances of safety and deliverance.

On the 15th of January, at night, a very large shark was observed swimming about us in a most ravenous manner, making attempts every now and then upon different parts of the boat, as if he would devour the very wood with hunger; he came several times and snapped at the steering oar, and even the stern-post.

We tried in vain to stab him with a lance, but were so weak as not to be able to make any impression upon his hard skin; he was so much larger than an ordinary one, and manifested such a fearless malignity, as to make us afraid of him; and our utmost efforts, which were at first directed to kill him for prey, became in the end self-defense. Baffled however in all his hungry attempts upon us, he shortly made off.

On the 16th of January, we were surrounded with porpoises in great numbers, that followed us nearly an hour, and which also defied all manoeuvres to catch them.

The 17th and 18th proved to be calm; and the distresses of a cheerless prospect and a burning hot sun, were again visited upon our devoted heads.

We began to think that Divine Providence had abandoned us at last; and it was but an unavailing effort to endeavour to prolong a now tedious existence. Horrible were the feelings that took possession of us! – The contemplation of a death of agony and torment, refined by the most dreadful and distressing reflections, absolutely prostrated both body and soul. There was not a hope now remaining to us but that which was derived from a sense of the mercies of our creator.

The night of the 18th was a despairing era in our sufferings; our minds were wrought up to the highest pitch of dread and apprehension for our fate, and all in them was dark, gloomy, and confused. About 8 o'clock, the terrible noise of whalespouts near us sounded in our ears: we could distinctly hear the furious thrashing of their tails in the water, and our weak minds pictured out their appalling and hideous aspects.

One of my companions, the black man, took an immediate fright, and solicited me to take out the oars, and endeavour to get away from them. I consented to his using any means for that purpose; but alas! It was wholly out of our power to raise a single arm in our own defense. Two or three of the whales came down near us, and went swiftly off across our stern, blowing and spouting at a terrible rate; they, however, after an hour or two disappeared, and we saw no more of them.

The next day, the 19th of January, we had extremely boisterous weather, with rain, heavy thunder and lightning, which reduced us again to the necessity of taking in all sail and lying to. The wind blew from every point of the compass within the twenty-four hours, and at last towards the next morning settled at E.NE. a strong breeze.

1821: WHALE-SHIP 'ESSEX'

January 20th

The black man, Richard Peterson, manifested today symptoms of a speedy dissolution; he had been lying between the seats in the boat, utterly dispirited and broken down, without being able to do the least duty, or hardly to place his hand to his head for the last three days, and had this morning made up his mind to die rather than endure further misery: he refused his allowance; said he was sensible of his approaching end, and was perfectly ready to die: in a few minutes he became speechless, the breath appeared to be leaving his body without producing the least pain, and at four o'clock he was gone.

I had two days previously, conversations with him on the subject of religion, on which he reasoned very sensibly, and with much composure; and begged me to let his wife know his fate, if ever I reached home in safety.

The next morning we committed him to the sea, in latitude 35°07' S. longitude 105°46' W.

The wind prevailed to the eastward until the 24th of January, when it again fell calm. We were now in a most wretched and sinking state of debility, hardly able to crawl around the boat, and possessing but strength enough to convey our scanty morsel to our mouths.

When I perceived this morning that it was calm, my fortitude almost forsook me. I thought to suffer another scorching day, like the last we had experienced, would close before night the scene of our miseries; and I felt many a despairing moment that day, that had well nigh proved fatal. It required an effort to look calmly forward, and contemplate what was yet in store for us, beyond what I felt I was capable of making; and what it was that buoyed me above all the terrors which surrounded us, God alone knows.

Our ounce and a half of bread, which was to serve us all day, was in some cases greedily devoured, as if life was to continue but another moment; and at other times, it was hoarded up and eaten crumb by crumb, at regular intervals during the day, as if it was to last us for ever.

To add to our calamities, biles began to break out upon us, and our imaginations shortly became as diseased as our bodies. I laid down at night to catch a few moments of oblivious sleep, and immediately my starving fancy was at work. I dreamt of being placed near a splendid and rich repast, where there was everything that the most dainty appetite could desire; and of contemplating the moment in which we were to commence to eat with enraptured feelings of delight; and just as I was about to partake of it, I suddenly awoke to the cold realities of my miserable situation. Nothing could have oppressed me so much. It set such a longing frenzy for victuals in my mind, that I felt as if I could have wished the dream to continue for ever, that I never might have awoke from it. I cast a sort of vacant stare about the boat, until my eyes rested upon a bit of tough cow-hide, which was fastened to one of the oars; I eagerly seized and commenced to chew it, but there was no substance in it, and it only served to fatigue my weak jaws, and add to my bodily pains.

My fellow sufferers murmured very much the whole time and continued to press me continually with questions upon the probability of our reaching land again. I kept constantly rallying my spirits to enable me to afford them comfort. I encouraged them to bear up against all evils, and if we must perish, to die in our own cause, and not weakly distrust the providence of the Almighty, by giving ourselves up to despair. I reasoned with them, and told them that we would not die sooner by keeping up our hopes; that the dreadful sacrifices and privations we endured were to preserve us from death, and were not to be put in competition with the price which we set upon our lives, and their value to our families; it was, besides, unmanly, to repine at what neither admitted of alleviation nor cure; and withal, that it was our solemn duty to recognize in our calamities an overruling divinity, by whose mercy we might be suddenly snatched from peril, and to rely upon him alone. "Who tempers the wind to the shorn lamb."

The three following days, the 25th, 26th, and 27th, were not distinguished by any particular circumstances. The wind still prevailed to the eastward, and by its obduracy, almost tore the very hopes of our hearts away: it was impossible to silence the rebellious repinings of our nature, at witnessing such a succession of hard fortune against us. It was our cruel lot not to have had one bright anticipation realized – not one wish of our thirsting souls gratified.

We had, at the end of these three days, been urged to the southward as far as latitude 36° into a chilly region, where rains and squalls prevailed; and we now calculated to tack and stand back to the northward: after much labour, we got our boat about; and so great was the fatigue attending this small exertion of our bodies, that we all gave up for a moment and abandoned her to her own course.

– Not one of us had now strength sufficient to steer, or indeed to make one single effort towards getting the sails properly trimmed, to enable us to make any headway. After an hour or two or relaxation, during which the horrors of our situation came upon us with a despairing force and effect, we made a sudden effort and got our sails into such a disposition, as that the boat would steer herself; and we then threw ourselves down awaiting the issue of time to bring us relief, or to take us from the scene of our troubles. We could now do nothing more; strength and spirits were totally gone; and what indeed could have been the narrow hopes, that in our situation, then bound us to life?

January 28th

Our spirits this morning were hardly sufficient to allow of our enjoying a change of the wind, which took place to the westward.—It had nearly become indifferent to us from what quarter it blew: nothing but the slight chance of meeting with a vessel remained to us now: it was this narrow comfort alone, that prevented me from lying down at once to die. But fourteen days' stinted allowance of provisions remained, and it was absolutely necessary to increase the quantity to enable us to live five days longer: we therefore partook of it, as pinching necessity demanded, and gave ourselves wholly up to the guidance and disposal of our Creator.

The 29th and 30th of January, the wind continued west, and we made considerable progress until the 31st, when it again came ahead, and prostrated all our hopes. On the 1st of February, it changed again to the westward, and on the 2nd and 3rd blew to the eastward; and we had it light and variable until the 8th of February.

Our sufferings were now drawing to a close; a terrible death appeared shortly to await us; hunger became violent and outrageous, and we prepared for a speedy release from our troubles; our speech and reason were both considerably impaired, and we were reduced to be at this time, certainly the most helpless and wretched of the whole human race.

Isaac Cole, one of our crew, had the day before this, in a fit of despair, thrown himself down in the boat, and was determined there calmly to wait for death. It was obvious that he had no chance; all was dark he said in his mind, not a single ray of hope was left for him to dwell upon; and it was folly and madness to be struggling against what appeared so palpably to be our fixed and settled destiny. I remonstrated with him as effectually as the weakness both of my body and understanding would allow of; and what I said appeared for a moment to have a considerable effect: he made a powerful and sudden effort, half rose up, crawled forward and hoisted the jib, and firmly and loudly cried that he would not give up; that he would live as long as the rest of us – but alas! this effort was but the hectic fever of the moment, and he shortly again relapsed into a state of melancholy and despair.

This day his reason was attacked, and he became about 9 o'clock in the morning a most miserable spectacle of madness: he spoke coherently about everything, calling loudly for a napkin and water, and then lying stupidly and senselessly down in the boat again, would close his hollow eyes, as if in death. About 10 o'clock, we suddenly perceived that he became speechless; we got him as well as we were able upon a board, placed on one of the seats of the boat, and covering him up with some old clothes, left him to his fate. He lay in the greatest pain and apparent misery, groaning piteously until four o'clock, when he died, in the most horrid and frightful convulsions I ever witnessed.

We kept his corpse all night, and in the morning my two companions began as of course to make preparations to dispose of it in the sea; when after reflecting on the subject all night, I addressed them on the painful subject of keeping the body for food!!

Our provisions could not possibly last us beyond three days, within which time it was not in any degree probable that we should find relief from our present sufferings, and that hunger would at last drive us to the necessity of casting lots. It was without any objection agreed to, and we set to work as fast as we were able to prepare it so as to prevent its spoiling.

We separated his limbs from his body, and cut all the flesh from the bones; after which, we opened the body, took out the heart, and then closed it again – sewed it up as decently as we could, and committed it to the sea.

We now first commenced to satisfy the immediately craving of nature from the heart, which we eagerly devoured, and then eat sparingly of a few pieces of the flesh; after which, we hung up the remainder, cut in thin strips about the boat, to dry in the sun: we made a fire and roasted some of it, to serve us during the next day.

In this manner did we dispose of our fellow-sufferer; the painful recollection of which, brings to mind at this moment, some of the most disagreeable and revolting ideas that it is capable of conceiving. We knew not then, to whose lot it would fall next, either to die or be shot, and eaten like the poor wretch we had just dispatched. Humanity must shudder at the dreadful recital. I have no language to paint the anguish of our souls in this dreadful dilemma.

The next morning, the 10th of February, we found that the flesh had become tainted, and had turned of a greenish colour, upon which we concluded to make a fire and cook it at once, to prevent its becoming so putrid as not to be eaten at all: we accordingly did so, and by that means preserved it for six or seven days longer; our bread during the time, remained untouched; as that would not be liable to spoil, we placed it carefully aside for the last moments of our trial.

About three o'clock this afternoon a strong breeze set in from the NW. and we made very good progress, considering that we were compelled to steer the boat by management of the sails alone: this wind continued until the thirteenth, when it changed again ahead. We contrived to keep soul and body together by sparingly partaking of our flesh, cut up in small pieces and eaten with salt-water.

By the fourteenth, our bodies became so far recruited, as to enable us to make a few attempts at guiding our boat again with the oar; by each taking his turn, we managed to effect it, and to make a tolerable good course.

On the fifteenth, our flesh was all consumed, and we were driven to the last morsel of bread, consisting of two cakes; our limbs had for the last two days swelled very much, and now began to pain us most excessively. We were still, as near as we could judge, three hundred miles from the land, and but three days of our allowance on hand. The hope of a continuation of the wind, which came out at west this morning, was the only comfort and solace that remained to us: so strong had our desires at last reached in this respect, that a high fever had set in, in our veins, and a longing that nothing but its continuation could satisfy. Matters were now with us at their height; all hope was cast upon the breeze; and we tremblingly and fearfully awaited its progress, and the dreadful development of our destiny.

On the sixteenth, at night, full of the horrible reflections of our situation, and panting with weakness, I laid down to sleep, almost indifferent whether I should ever see the light again. I had not lain long, before I dreamt I saw a ship at some distance off from us, and strained every nerve to get to her, but could not.

I awoke almost overpowered with the frenzy I had caught in my slumbers, and stung with the cruelties of a diseased and disappointed imagination.

On the seventeenth, in the afternoon, a heavy cloud appeared to be settling down in an E. by N. direction from us, which in my view, indicated the vicinity of some land, which I took for the island of Massafuera. I concluded it could be no other; and immediately upon this reflection, the life blood began to flow again briskly in my veins. I told my companions that I was well convinced it was land, and if so, in all probability we would reach it before two days more.

My words appeared to comfort them much; and by repeated assurances of the favourable appearance of things, their spirits acquired even a degree of elasticity that was truly astonishing. The dark features of our distress began now to diminish a little, and the countenance, even amid the gloomy bodings of our hard lot, to assume a much fresher hue. We directed our course for the cloud, and our progress that night was extremely good.

The next morning, before daylight, Thomas Nicholson, a boy about seventeen years of age, one of my two companions who had thus far survived with me, after having bailed the boat, laid down, drew a piece of canvass over him, and cried out, that he then wished to die immediately. I saw that he had given up, and I attempted to speak a few words of comfort and encouragement to him, and endeavoured to persuade him that it was a great weakness and even wickedness to abandon a reliance upon the Almighty, while the least hope, and a breath of life remained; but he felt unwilling to listen to any of the consolatory suggestions which I made to him; and, notwithstanding the extreme probability, which I stated there was of our gaining the land before the end of two days more, he insisted upon lying down and giving himself up to despair.

A fixed look of settled and forsaken despondency came over his face: he lay for some time silent, sullen, and sorrowful – and I felt at once satisfied, that the coldness of death was fast gathering upon him: there was a sudden and unaccountable earnestness in his manner, that alarmed me, and made me fear that I myself might unexpectedly be overtaken by a like weakness, or dizziness of nature, that would bereave me at once of both reason and life, but Providence willed it otherwise.

At about seven o'clock this morning, while I was lying asleep, my companion who was steering, suddenly and loudly called out, "There's a Sail!" I know not what was the first movement I made upon hearing such an unexpected cry: the earliest of my recollections are, that immediately I stood up, gazing in a state of abstraction and ecstasy upon the blessed vision of a vessel about seven miles off from us; she was standing in the same direction with us, and the only sensation I felt at the moment was, that of a violent and unaccountable impulse to fly directly towards her.

I do not believe it is possible to form a just conception of the pure, strong feelings, and the unmingled emotions of joy and gratitude, that took possession of my mind on this occasion: the boy, too, took a sudden and animated start from his despondency, and stood up to witness the probable instrument of his salvation.

Our only fear was now, that she would not discover us, or that we might not be able to intercept her course: we, however, put our boat immediately, as well as we were able, in a direction to cut her off; and found, to our great joy, that we sailed faster than she did.

Upon observing us, she shortened sail, and allowed us to come up to her. The captain hailed us and asked who we were. I told him we were from a wreck, and he cried out immediately for us to come alongside the ship. I made an effort to assist myself along to the side, for the purpose of getting up, but strength failed me altogether, and I found it impossible to move a step further without help.

We must have formed at that moment, in the eyes of the captain and his crew, a most deplorable and affecting picture of suffering and misery. Our cadaverous countenances, sunken eyes, and bones just starting through our skin, with the ragged remnants of clothes stuck about our sun-burnt bodies, must have produced an appearance to him affecting and revolting in the highest degree.

The sailors commenced to remove us from our boat, and we were taken to the cabin, and comfortably provided for in every respect. In a few minutes we were permitted to taste of a little thin food, made from tapiocha, and in a few days with prudent management, we were considerably recruited.

This vessel proved to be the brig Indian, captain William Crozier, of London; to whom we are indebted for every polite, friendly, and attentive disposition towards us, that can possibly characterize a man of humanity and feeling. We were taken up in latitude 33°45' S. longitude 81°03' W.

At twelve o'clock this day we saw the island of Massafuera, and on the 25th of February, we arrived at Valparaiso in utter distress and poverty. Our wants were promptly relieved there.

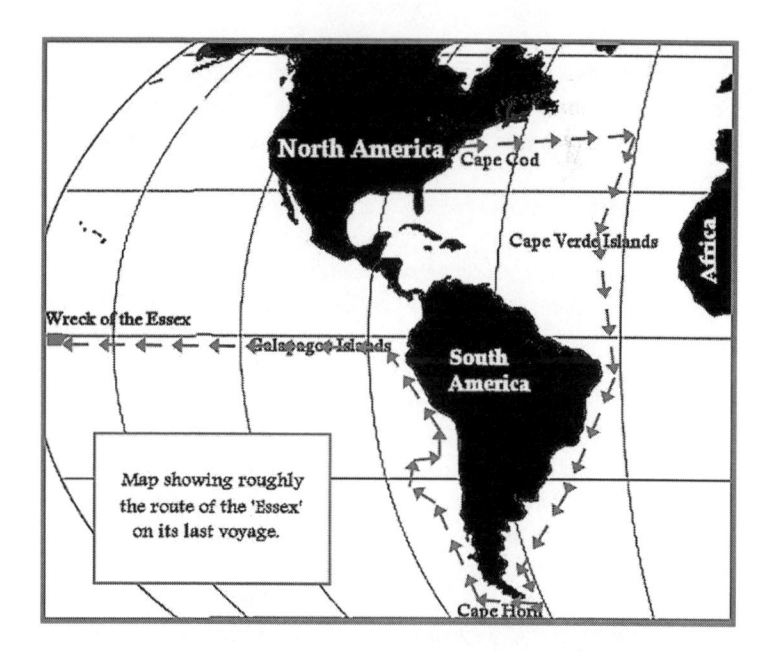

Map showing roughly the route of the 'Essex' on its last voyage.

*

The captain and the survivors of this boat's crew, were taken up by the American whale-ship, the Dauphin, Captain Zimri Coffin, of Nantucket, and arrived at Valparaiso on the seventeenth of March following: he was taken up in latitude 37° S. off the island of St. Mary. The third boat got separated from him on the 28th of January, and has not been heard of since.

The names of all the survivors, are as follows — Captain George Pollard, junr. Charles Ramsdale, Owen Chase, Benjamin Lawrence, and Thomas Nicholson, all of Nantucket. There died in the captain's boat, the following: Brazilla Ray of Nantucket, Owen Coffin of the same place, who was shot, and Samuel Reed, a black.

The captain relates, that after being separated, as herein before stated, they continued to make what progress they could towards the island of Juan Fernandez, as was agreed upon; but contrary winds and the extreme debility of the crew prevailed against their united exertions. He was with us equally surprised and concerned at the separation that took place between us; but continued on his course, almost confident of meeting with us again.

On the fourteenth, the whole stock of provisions belonging to the second mate's boat, was entirely exhausted, and on the twenty-fifth, the black man, Lawsen Thomas, died, and was eaten by his surviving companions.

On the twenty-first, the captain and his crew were in the like dreadful situation with respect to their provisions; and on the twenty-third, another coloured man, Charles Shorter, died out of the same boat, and his body was shared for food between the crews of both boats.

On the twenty-seventh, another, Isaac Shepherd (a black man), died in the third boat; and on the twenty-eight, another black, named Samuel Reed, died out of the captain's boat. The bodies of these men constituted their only food while it lasted; and on the twenty-ninth, owing to the darkness of the night and want of sufficient power to manage their boats, those of the captain and second mate separated in latitude 35° S. longitude 100° W. on the 1st of February, having consumed the last morsel, the captain and the three other men that remained with him, were reduced to the necessity of casting lots. It fell upon Owen Coffin to die, who with great fortitude and resignation submitted to his fate. They drew lots to see who should shoot him: he placed himself firmly to receive his death, and was immediately shot by Charles Ramsdale, whose hard fortune it was to become his executioner.

On the 11th, Brazilla Ray died; and on these two bodies the captain and Charles Ramsdale, the only two that were then left, subsisted until the morning of the twenty-third, when they fell in with the ship Dauphin, as before stated, and were snatched from impending destruction. Every assistance and attentive humanity, was bestowed upon them by Capt. Coffin, to whom Capt. Pollard acknowledged every grateful obligation.

Upon making known the fact, that three of our companions had been left at Ducies Island, to the captain of the U.S. frigate Constellation, which lay at Valparaiso when we arrived, he said he should immediately take measures to have them taken off.

*

On the 11th of June following I arrived at Nantucket in the whale-ship the Eagle, Capt. William H. Coffin. My family had received the most distressing account of our shipwreck, and had given me up for lost.

My unexpected appearance was welcomed with the most grateful obligations and acknowledgments to a beneficent Creator, who had guided me through darkness, trouble, and death, once more to the bosom of my country and friends.

SUPPLEMENT

The following is a list of the whole crew of the ship, with their arrangements into the three several boats upon starting from the wreck: the names of those who died, were left on the island, or shot – with those also who survived, and who were in the third or second mate's boat at the time of separation – and whose fate is yet uncertain:

Capt. James Pollard, Jun. 17, 1st boat, survived
Obed Hendricks, 1st boat, put in 3rd boat
Brazilla Ray, 1st boat, died
Owen Coffin, 1st boat, shot
Samuel Reed (black), 1st boat, died
Charles Ramsdale, 1st boat, survived
Seth Weeks, 1st boat, left on the island
Owen Chase, 2nd boat, survived
Benjamin Lawrence, 2nd boat, survived
Thomas Nicholson, 2nd boat, survived
Isaac Cole, 2nd boat, survived
Richard Peterson (black), 2nd boat, survived
William Wright, 2nd boat, left on the island
Matthew P. Joy, 3rd boat, died
Thomas Chapple, 3rd boat, left on the island
Joseph West, 3rd boat, missing
Lawson Thomas (black), 3rd boat, died
Charles Shorter (black), 3rd boat, died
Isaiah Shepherd (black), 3rd boat, died
William Bond (black), 3rd boat, missing
FINIS.

APPENDICES

1. Preface to 1821 Edition

The increasing attention which is bestowed upon the whale fishery in the United States, has lately caused a very considerable commercial excitement; and no doubt it will become, if it be not at present, as important and general a branch of commerce as any belonging to our country. It is now principally confined to a very industrious and enterprising portion of the population of the States, many individuals of whom have amassed very rapid and considerable fortunes. It has enriched the inhabitants without bringing with it the usual corruptions and luxuries of a foreign trade; and those who are now most successful and conspicuous in it, are remarkable for the primitive simplicity, integrity, and hospitality of the island. This trade, if I may so call it, took its rise amongst the earliest settlers, and has gradually advanced to the extended, important, and lucrative state in which it now is, without any material interruption, and with very little competition until the present time. The late war temporally, but in a great degree affected its prosperity, by subjecting numerous fine vessels with their cargoes to capture and loss; but in its short continuance, it was not sufficient to divert the enterprise of the whalemen, nor to subdue the active energies of the capitalists embarked in it. At the conclusion of peace, those energies burst out afresh; and our sails now almost whiten the distant confines of the Pacific.

The English have a few ships there; and the advantages which they possess over ours, it may be feared will materially affect our success, by producing in time a much more extensive and powerful competition. They are enabled to realize a greater profit from the demand and price of oil in their markets; and the encouragement afforded by parliament, not only in permitting the importation of it free of duty, but in granting a liberal bounty.

Recent events have shown that we require a competent naval force in the Pacific, for the protection of this important and lucrative branch of commerce; for the want of which, many serious injuries and insults have been lately received, which have a tendency to retard its flourishing progress, and which have proved of serious consequence to the parties concerned.

During the late war, the exertions and intrepidity of Capt. Porter, were the means of saving a great deal of valuable property, which otherwise must have fallen into the hands of the enemy. His skilful, spirited, and patriotic conduct, on all occasions where he was called upon to act, imparted a protection and confidence to our countrymen, which completely fulfilled their expectations of him, and without doubt those of the government in sending him there.

Our ships usually occupy from two to three years in making a voyage. Occasionally, necessity obliges them to go into port for provisions, water, and repairs – in some cases, amongst mere savages, and in others, inhospitable people, from whom they are liable to every species of fraud, imposition, and force, which require some competent power to awe and redress. As long as the struggle between the patriots and royalists continues, or even should that speedily end – as long as young and instable governments, as there naturally must be for many years to come, exist there, our whalemen will continue to require that countenance and support which the importance and prosperity of the trade to them, and to the country, eminently entitle them. It is, undoubtedly, a most hazardous business, involving many incidental and unavoidable sacrifices, the severity of which it seems cruel to increase by the neglect or refusal of a proper protection.

The seamen employed in the fishery, and particularly those from Nantucket, are composed of the sons and connexions of the most respectable families on the island; and, unlike the majority of the class or profession to which they belong, they labour not only for their temporary subsistence, but they have an ambition and pride among them which seeks after distinguishment and promotion. Almost all of them enter the service with views of a future command; and submit cheerfully to the hardships and drudgery of the intermediate stations, until they become thoroughly acquainted with their business.

There are common sailors, boat-steerers, and harpooners: the last of these is the most honourable and important. It is in this station, that all the capacity of the young sailor is elicited; on the dexterous management of the harpoon, the line, and the lance, and in the adventurous positions which he takes alongside of his enemy, depends almost entirely the successful issue of his attack; and more real chivalry is not often exhibited on the deck of a battleship, than is displayed by these hardy sons of the ocean, in some of their gallant exploits among the whales. Nursed in the dangers of their business, and exposed to the continual hazards and hardships of all seasons, climates, and weathers, it will not be surprising if they should become a fearless set of people, and pre-eminent in all the requisites of good seamen. Two voyages are generally considered sufficient to qualify an active and intelligent young man for command; in which time, he learns from experience, and the examples which are set him, all that is necessary to be known.

While on this subject, I may be allowed to observe that it would not be an unprofitable task in a majority of our respectable shipmasters in the merchant service, to look into the principles of conduct, and study the economical management of the captains of our whale-ships. I am confident many serviceable hints could be gathered from the admirable system by which they regulate their concerns. They would learn, also, what respect is due to the character and standing of a captain of a whale-ship, which those of the merchant service affect so much to undervalue. If the post of danger be the post of honour; and if merit emanates from exemplary private character, uncommon intelligent, and professional gallantry, then is it due to a great majority of the shipmasters of Nantucket, that they should be held above the operations of an invidious and unjust distinction? It is a curious fact that one does exist; and it is equally an illiberal, as an undeserved reproach upon them, which time and an acquaintance with their merits must speedily wipe away.

2. 'Gothic Non-Fiction'

Chase might not have proved himself to be the greatest of writers. His aim in writing was a modest one: to earn a little remuneration to compensate him for his losses. But to the reader with an interest in genre and literary history his brief account has an interest that goes beyond its subject matter.

Two years earlier, Shelley had written her novel 'Frankenstein'. Two decades earlier, Coleridge had written his narrative poem 'The Rime of The Ancient Mariner'. Both works were Romantic reimaginings of Gothic themes. Both were of course fictional. What makes Chase's book so fascinating is the fact that he has created a story that is just as horrific and macabre but is entirely factual (albeit from one man's perspective).

When, in 1777, Clara Reeves reworked 'The Castle of Otranto' to make it more realistic there were concerns expressed that readers might mistake 'The English Baron' as fact and become unreasonably frightened. Chase's work is evidence that these concerns were fair. Its barely adorned realism and avoidance of hyperbole really do make the tale more terrible than fiction. It also demonstrates that the converse could be true: a true account that is overly descriptive in style could be mistaken for fiction. His narrative achieves a balance between opposing styles of writing that makes the finished work moving, frightening, and credible.

We believe this:

> *We separated his limbs from his body, and cut all the flesh from the bones; after which, we opened the body, took out the heart, and then closed it again – sewed it up as decently as we could, and committed it to the sea. (Chase)*

But not this:

> *I collected bones from charnel houses and disturbed, with profane fingers, the tremendous secrets of the human frame. […] The dissecting room and the slaughter-house furnished many of my materials; and often did my human nature turn with loathing from my occupation. (Shelley)*

Frankenstein, the fictional character, moralises to a far greater degree than does Chase. Both are, at these moments in their narratives, 'pale' and 'cadaverous' in appearance. Chase due to starvation and Frankenstein due to confinement.

Confinement is another Gothic motif. It's appropriate and very sad that both Chase and Pollard ended their lives in a way that showed again reality echoing imagination. Pollard was shipwrecked in his next voyage too and did not return to the sea. Every 20th November he would confine himself to one room and not eat or drink to remember the crew that died. Chase suffered from a mental disorder which today might be diagnosed as post-traumatic stress. He would lock himself away in the room at the top of his house. Upon his death the attic was found to contain food that he had been buying and hoarding for years.

In the next section is Coleridge's 'The Rime of The Ancient Mariner'. Like 'Frankenstein' this narrative has an overt moral lesson. Chase tends not to moralise. However he does at one point hint at a private realisation that his harpoon had caused the tragedy: 'He came directly from the shoal which we had just before entered, and in which we had struck three of his companions, as if fired with revenge for their sufferings.'   JT

3. *From* The Rime of the Ancient Mariner
   S T Coleridge 1798

Part III

There passed a weary time. Each throat
Was parched, and glazed each eye.
A weary time! a weary time!
How glazed each weary eye,

When looking westward, I beheld
A something in the sky.

At first it seemed a little speck,
And then it seemed a mist;
It moved and moved, and took at last
A certain shape, I wist.

A speck, a mist, a shape, I wist!
And still it neared and neared:
As if it dodged a water-sprite,
It plunged and tacked and veered.

With throats unslaked, with black lips baked,
We could nor laugh nor wail;
Through utter drought all dumb we stood!
I bit my arm, I sucked the blood,
And cried, A sail! a sail!

With throats unslaked, with black lips baked,
Agape they heard me call:
Gramercy! they for joy did grin,
And all at once their breath drew in.
As they were drinking all.

See! see! (I cried) she tacks no more!
Hither to work us weal;
Without a breeze, without a tide,
She steadies with upright keel!

The western wave was all a-flame.
The day was well nigh done!
Almost upon the western wave
Rested the broad bright Sun;
When that strange shape drove suddenly
Betwixt us and the Sun.

And straight the Sun was flecked with bars,
(Heaven's Mother send us grace!)
As if through a dungeon-grate he peered
With broad and burning face.

Alas! (thought I, and my heart beat loud)
How fast she nears and nears!
Are those *her* sails that glance in the Sun,
Like restless gossameres?

Are those her *ribs* through which the Sun
Did peer, as through a grate?

APPENDIX

And is that Woman all her crew?
Is that a DEATH? and are there two?
Is DEATH that woman's mate?

Her lips were red, *her* looks were free,
Her locks were yellow as gold:
Her skin was as white as leprosy,
The Night-mare LIFE-IN-DEATH was she,
Who thicks man's blood with cold.

The naked hulk alongside came,
And the twain were casting dice;
'The game is done! I've won! I've won!'
Quoth she, and whistles thrice.

The Sun's rim dips; the stars rush out;
At one stride comes the dark;
With far-heard whisper, o'er the sea,
Off shot the spectre-bark.

We listened and looked sideways up!
Fear at my heart, as at a cup,
My life-blood seemed to sip!
The stars were dim, and thick the night,
The steersman's face by his lamp gleamed white;
From the sails the dew did drip—
Till clomb above the eastern bar
The hornèd Moon, with one bright star
Within the nether tip.

One after one, by the star-dogged Moon,
Too quick for groan or sigh,
Each turned his face with a ghastly pang,
And cursed me with his eye.

Four times fifty living men,
(And I heard nor sigh nor groan)

With heavy thump, a lifeless lump,
They dropped down one by one.

The souls did from their bodies fly,—
They fled to bliss or woe!
And every soul, it passed me by,
Like the whizz of my cross-bow!

Part IV

'I fear thee, ancient Mariner!
I fear thy skinny hand!
And thou art long, and lank, and brown,
As is the ribbed sea-sand.

I fear thee and thy glittering eye,
And thy skinny hand, so brown.'—
Fear not, fear not, thou Wedding-Guest!
This body dropt not down.

Alone, alone, all, all alone,
Alone on a wide wide sea!
And never a saint took pity on
My soul in agony.

The many men, so beautiful!
And they all dead did lie:
And a thousand thousand slimy things
Lived on; and so did I.

I looked upon the rotting sea,
And drew my eyes away;
I looked upon the rotting deck,
And there the dead men lay.

APPENDIX

I looked to heaven, and tried to pray;
But or ever a prayer had gusht,
A wicked whisper came, and made
My heart as dry as dust.

I closed my lids, and kept them close,
And the balls like pulses beat;
For the sky and the sea, and the sea and the sky
Lay dead like a load on my weary eye,
And the dead were at my feet.

The cold sweat melted from their limbs,
Nor rot nor reek did they:
The look with which they looked on me
Had never passed away.

An orphan's curse would drag to hell
A spirit from on high;
But oh! more horrible than that
Is the curse in a dead man's eye!
Seven days, seven nights, I saw that curse,
And yet I could not die.

The moving Moon went up the sky,
And no where did abide:
Softly she was going up,
And a star or two beside—

Her beams bemocked the sultry main,
Like April hoar-frost spread;
But where the ship's huge shadow lay,
The charmèd water burnt alway
A still and awful red.

Beyond the shadow of the ship,
I watched the water-snakes:
They moved in tracks of shining white,

And when they reared, the elfish light
Fell off in hoary flakes.

Within the shadow of the ship
I watched their rich attire:
Blue, glossy green, and velvet black,
They coiled and swam; and every track
Was a flash of golden fire.

O happy living things! no tongue
Their beauty might declare:
A spring of love gushed from my heart,
And I blessed them unaware:
Sure my kind saint took pity on me,
And I blessed them unaware.

The self-same moment I could pray;
And from my neck so free
The Albatross fell off, and sank
Like lead into the sea.

Printed in Great Britain
by Amazon